A Pig in a Passage

A
Pig
in a
Passage

ANN DRYSDALE

ROBERT HALE · LONDON

© Ann Drysdale 1997
First published in Great Britain 1997

ISBN 0 7090 6077 7

Robert Hale Limited
Clerkenwell House
Clerkenwell Green
London EC1R OHT

2   4   6   8   10   9   7   5   3   1

Photoset in North Wales by
Derek Doyle & Associates, Mold, Flintshire.
Printed in Great Britain by
St Edmundsbury Press Limited, Bury St Edmunds
and bound by
WBC Book Manufacturers Limited, Bridgend.

Contents

Nothing more certain than incertainties;
Fortune is full of fresh variety:
Constant in nothing but inconstancy.

The Shepherd's Content, Richard Barnfield (1574–1627)

Felix qui potuit rerum cognoscere causas.
                              Georgics ii, 490 Virgil

Cetera quis nescit?

                              Amores I.v.25 Ovid

Acknowledgements

The author acknowledges permission to include copyright material by other writers. Thanks are due to Diana Hendry and Peterloo Poets for lines from 'Solo', in her collection 'Making Blue', to Special Rider Music/Sony/ATV Music Publishing for lines from 'Baby, I'm in the Mood for You' by Bob Dylan and the Estate of Robert Frost and Jonathan Cape Ltd for a line from 'Mending Wall' from *The Poetry of Robert Frost* edited by Edward Connery Lathem. Also to Carcanet Press for lines from Robert Graves's 'To Walk on Hills' from *The Centenary Selected Poems*, 1995, and to B. Feldman and Co. Ltd, trading as Trident Music, for extracts from 'The Prophet's Song' by Brian May and 'Love Of My Life' and 'Bohemian Rhapsody' by Freddie Mercury. The shades of quoted writers whose work is no longer in copyright are invoked and blessed. Unattributed poems are the author's own.

The author gratefully acknowledges the assistance of the Arts Council of Wales, whose generosity bought the time needed to complete the work.

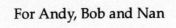

For Andy, Bob and Nan

Foreword

That Ann Drysdale would ever leave Hagg House Farm
was unthinkable, but it was not the tough, relentless work
that drove her away, nor was it a lack of money. It was the
invasion of her precious hard-won privacy by strangers in
a caravan.

In this poetic and moving story, she chronicles those
delightful but extremely sorrowful final months. I loved
Turpin the dog who helped at the birth of piglets and
brought the pet rabbit home at night; I cheered her achievement in becoming a true moorland sheep farmer with her
moving account of the death of a favourite ewe and I chuck-
led at her struggles with contraptions like supermops,
electrical apparatus and motor bikes and at her granddad's
difficulty in a field at night, trying to distinguish a cow clap
from his flat cap. And now I know why vets wear brown
overalls.

Just as Ann Drysdale wept at the unjustified intrusion of
strangers into her world, so you'll weep with both sorrow
and joy as her dream slowly disintegrates and she accepts
the inevitable – that she must leave Hagg House Farm, her
animals and the source of so many precious memories.

Nicholas Rhea

Introduction

There were four of us, up to our wellington-tops in the sort of mixture of mud and cattle effluent that farmers call slurry. Jim and his sons George and Sid were there, and I, and the vet expected at any moment.

Jim's herd of hill cows were well on the way to becoming accredited – that is declared free of brucellosis, or contagious abortion. They had passed a series of six-monthly tests. The few positive reactors had been weeded out and from now on they were to be tested only annually.

And this was the day. It had taken us all our guile and cunning to gather the canny old beasts together and drive them on to the big covered yard behind Jim's house, where he had erected a race and a crush for the occasion, and now they were careering around like Bacchantes, careless of their comfort and our safety. Those who had been here before were furious because they knew what was coming, those who hadn't were panic-stricken because they didn't.

All was noise and confusion. The hollow bellows of the swing-titted, saggy-bellied beasts rolled around under the corrugated iron roof and threatened to deafen me while paradoxically amplifying the curses of the three jolly farmers who staggered and cavorted in the glutinous muck.

Had we all lived a little nearer sea level, and had these been dairy cows, used to twice-daily contact with the human race and resigned to the fact that their calves, after the first few days, were a luxury to be heard, but not seen, sniffed or suckled, the testing job would have been a doddle. As it was, they were rough, tough hill cows, Limousin crosses for the most part, Jim having given in to fashion, who had wintered outdoors and calved in sheltered corners around the perimeter of the farm.

Red-haired and wild-eyed, they kicked and plunged as we moved among them, sorting out the calves and shoving them outside through the double doors. They were too young to be tested and their presence was an additional inconvenience. Jim and George, shouting and flailing about like a couple of berserk windmills, would cut out a calf and head it towards the doors. When it was almost there, I would haul back the door and the calf, blinking in the shaft of sudden sunshine, would trot outside while Sid leapt in behind it to prevent its mother from following until I had slid the great door shut again.

Well, that was it in theory. When tested under field conditions, however, the procedure as laid down left much to be desired. Time and again, when I opened the door, the wailing throng of calves assembled outside would rush it in an attempt to rejoin their mothers, so that I had to slam it in the face of the one who was in the process of being ejected. Each time this happened it would become warier of approaching the door and its mother more alarmed and convinced that it was in danger.

And as more calves were inveigled outside, more cows tried to get to them each time the door was opened. At last one enraged old lady whose calf's note of distress hovered in descant above the rest, made a now-or-never bid for freedom. 'Turn 'er! Turn 'er,' shouted George and Jim. 'Yee-har,' shouted Sid, leaping in front of her with his arms raised above his head, so that he was in no position to save himself when she came on regardless and he was pitched over backwards into the receiving clarts.

I shut the door, but not until after the cow had bolted, and went to give Sid a hand up.

But George got there first. He bestrode his fallen brother like a bantam cock straddling a defeated rival. 'You useless bugger,' he crowed, grinning. 'You couldn't turn a pig in a passage!'

I am ashamed to say, I laughed. At George, ludicrous in triumph; at Sid, ludicrous in defeat. At the whole stupid carry-on and the deadly seriousness with which four shit-blitzed adults played tag with enraged cattle who themselves presented a risible spectacle when putting themselves to their speed, so that everything that should hang, swung. But most of all I laughed at the delightful thought of Sid, or anyone else for that matter, trying to turn a pig in a passage.

I should have held my mirth. It was not long before I, too, was upended in the mire, and the same accusation was levelled at me.

When all the calves were safely outside, and the vet had arrived and had his cup of tea, the testing procedure began in earnest. Along one side of the yard, Jim had constructed a race – a fenced-off passage too narrow for a cow to turn round, into which they would be driven in turn, up to a crush gate at the end through which they would put their heads, whereupon someone – I in this case – would pull a lever and nip the bars together just tight enough so that their heads were held painlessly fast.

Not that the old girls didn't kick a bit when they realized they were ensnared, but after a moment or two they would calm down and the vet would go into the race and draw a sample of blood from a vein in their tails. This procedure in itself was not without hazard, since the poor animals, trapped as they were, had only their anal sphincters with which to register their displeasure. Not for nothing did the vet wear a brown overall.

I would write down the eartag number of each cow as I snared it, match it to the number on the sample bottle and fill in sundry other details about her. One of the things I had to log was her age. 'How old?' I'd say to Jim and he would utter, straightfaced, the first number that came into his head. Thus although I never made a mistake in relating individual cows to their particular samples, I found myself wishing that I had a little of that magical elixir with which Jim must dose them to keep number 350 frozen at the age of five for three years running and to enable number 222 who, to my knowledge, had seen at least seven summers, to slide annually backwards into a fast-approaching adolescence. And the vet, although he must have noticed, never said a word.

But oh, how I loved testing days. The sound and the smell and the being one of the lads. The proximity of the beasts and the trust placed in me to get the paper work right. I had worked nearly twenty years to be part of that precious team, to be certain that I would be called upon to go to Jim's farm and George's when the calls came from the Ministry that it was time for testing the cattle or counting the sheep, to be sure that I would be asked to take part in haymaking, gathering or clipping. And even at the end I never felt entirely secure, still longed for the comfort of being taken for granted.

That night, at home alone, I replayed and reorchestrated the proceedings in my head, gently filing down the uncomfortable moments so that they no longer stood proud of the smoothness of the day. Mistakes and triumphs cancelled each other out until at the end that delicious phrase stood out alone, like the bead of sweat on the end of Jim's nose when the stampede was at its height. A pig in a passage.

Oh, I could see it. A great spotted sow, bearing down at full tilt.

I could see the passage, too. Damp and ill-lit, leading past closed doors to a small scullery out of which someone must have shooed the disgruntled animal.

On she came, her bristly sides brushing the pale green paint on the passage walls, her splayed feet clacketting on the brown linoleum, making for the front door which stood half open at my back.

And I knew that if that pig wanted out of that door, there wasn't a damned thing I could do about it.

1

A Cold Coming

When blizzards blow under the tiles
And the dishcloth crisps on the draining-board
And the snowscape stretches for miles and miles
And only the idiot ventures abroad,
When it's early to bed, and thank heavens for that,
Then coldly keens the cast-out cat:
Miaow! Miaow!—a doleful din
And who will rise and let him in?

When slippery stones by the pond
Make filling a bucket an effort of will
And you're walled-up for weeks in the back of beyond
In a farm at the foot of a hell of a hill,
Then it's early to bed, and thank heavens for that,
Till coldly keens the cast-out cat:
Miaow! Miaow!—a doleful din
And who will rise and let him in?

Christmas 1984. It began to snow about lunchtime. I had
been up on the moor to check the sheep and the first cold,
wet whiskers of it tickled the back of my neck as I satisfied
myself that they were all munching contentedly and show-

ing no signs of straying in among the neighbour's group over the next hill.

These were the young sheep, learning for the first time to stick to their own special routine which would ensure their safety if and when the weather got really bad.

Each farmer turns his young female sheep – the gimmer hoggs – out on the hill at this time of year and there are always half a dozen grazing groups, each watched over by a fussing shepherd, on the great moor above the house during the hours of daylight.

With the typical perversity of the hill farmer, these precious flocks are watched over, brought in at night, and encouraged to stay near their home until the end of March, when they are dogged and harried as far up the moor as they'll go, to encourage them to make the best use of their 'stint'.

This process is called 'hefting'. It is quite fun in clement weather, but hard on the wellingtons.

All was well with my flock, so I turned up my collar and headed for home. There were fresh tyre marks on the whitened road and the gate stood open. Someone had driven down. And I shut the gate angrily, breaking into a jog-trot in my haste to get back and find out who this thoughtless visitor might be.

When I came to the top of the hill above the house, I saw a most amazing sight. There, freewheeling backwards and running forwards in alternate fits and starts in an attempt to get back up the slippery lane, was a fat, black Austin taxi-cab.

I took a firmer grip on the bundle of heather twigs I had brought back to light the fire and stared harder, unable to believe my eyes.

But sure enough, there it was, bringing back the sight and sound of damp, wintry London streets, big stores and Christmas shopping in the West End, where little last-minute gifts could be made special by some particularly prestigious paper bag.

The diesel engine throbbed and the great black tortoise lurched forward again, the 'For Hire' sign glowing orange in the grey, flurrying afternoon.

For a moment the unreality persisted, then suddenly all was clear. Up the road behind the taxi, obviously all ready to offer a friendly shove, strode a tall, gangling figure, and in that moment Christmas, which had been somehow hanging fire, really began.

For under the punk haircut, inside the army surplus overcoat and above the big Doc Marten boots with the scarlet laces, was Andy, my own beloved elder son.

I shouted a greeting and ran to meet him. The snow turned to a misty drizzle. At the same time the taxi, with a last mighty effort, gained the top of the hill and disappeared on its way back to Northallerton.

The Christmas holidays came to an end; the boys went back. Robert to his boarding school in York and Andy to his polytechnic in London. They left behind an assortment of memories which I found when I looked back, sweet and fuzzy like a fistful of unwrapped sweets fished out of a forgotten pocket.

The lavatory cistern was once more *hors de combat* and each time I climbed up on to the seat and reached into the icy water to tweak the bit of electric fence wire that was once again the only way to trigger the flush, I was reminded of their fleeting visit and of the transience of technology.

Mind you, it was technology that had saved our Christmas dinner. We had all turned up at my mother's house, by invitation, appetites agog, to discover that the preparations weren't as far advanced as Mother had given us to believe.

She had a comprehensive collection of kitchen gadgetry, including a fine new cooker, one of the sort that has a double oven. Hours earlier, she had put the turkey into the bottom oven and the plates to warm in the top one. But, catering most of the time for only two and using only the top oven, this was the one she had switched on. When she came to baste the turkey it was still raw. Cold to the touch. Poor Mum was near to tears.

We all did our best to cheer her up, saying we didn't mind a bit. Looking round her wonderful kitchen, so different from our own, Andy suggested the microwave. After all, that's what it was for, he reasoned. Thawing things out and cooking them fast. We found the handbook and the bird-roasting instructions. My daughter Nan read them out aloud and Andy did a simultaneous translation into terminology that we could transpose into action. The logic and the maths involved seemed deep.

We put the turkey into the microwave, shut the door and pressed the buttons. Countdown accomplished, we waited for lift off. Nothing.

The trouble was that food in a microwave has to revolve on an inner turntable and turkeys, having been invented some time earlier, are basically longer than they are wide, with projecting parts that prevent them from turning round in a confined space.

Nothing daunted, Andy and I set to re-truss the bird in the lotus position, binding it tightly across the breast with hairy string. When it was eventually laid out on the serving dish it was perfectly cooked, but round, pale and unbrowned. When we removed the string it looked exactly like a big bare bottom. It seemed almost cruel to carve it.

The vegetables were a little past their best when we finally sat down to eat, but the plates were wonderfully hot. 'Never mind,' I said, as the first slices of meat were handed round. 'Everything is for the best in the best of all possible worlds.' But nobody got the joke.

It snowed again and the world went white. Not in time for Christmas, which would have made it an acceptable martyrdom, but just in time to make the going-back of the boys that little bit more of a circus than usual.

Andy was finding his feet in London. He had made friends and saw in them the makings of a band, so he planned to take Boris back to London with him. Boris was his beloved bass guitar which had become almost a part of him in his last years in school. But with Boris had to go his life support system – a huge Peavey amplifier and two large and unwieldy speakers.

No real problem – we had established that British Rail parcels would deal with it. But because of the snow the first step, that of getting it all to the station, took on all the orchestrated drama of a polar expedition.

In a blizzard, we loaded the carefully-wrapped parcels into the transport box attached to the hydraulic linkage on Jim's tractor and ferried them carefully to the ancient store-all hen-hut at the top of the hill, where we stowed them safe. No taxi would get down the lane to the house, but the snow-plough had been along the top road the night before and we reckoned a driver who knew the way would make it that far, not without difficulty but certainly without danger.

At the pre-arranged time, Andy and I carted his suitcases up to the road and waited. And waited.

Almost twenty minutes after he should have been on his way, we heard a voice calling my name. The lady who drives the taxi was struggling along the road in wellingtons, waving and shouting. She had got to the last steep hill half a mile away and had had to abandon the car. Knowing that we were waiting she had come on to let us know and help us carry the cases back to it. If we made haste Andy could still catch his train, and he resigned himself, sadly but without complaint, to leaving his beloved Boris behind.

And then I got angry. Angry and sad, because I felt I had somehow let Andy down. I had no time to go and borrow the tractor again. No time to go back to the taxi and push it up the hill – but I was damned if I was going to be beaten by what amounted, by local standards, to a piffling quantity of snow.

I got some plastic fertilizer bags from the hen-hut and made holes in them with a pair of rusty sheep-shears. I threaded baler band through and looped it into makeshift traces, and the three of us – Andy and I and Marge-the-taxi, a mother herself who understood the instinctive application of discretionary effort, hauled the whole issue along the unbroken ridge of piled snow in the middle of the road.

After I had waved Andy on his way and watched until the taxi was safely out of sight, I wandered slowly home, wondering whether this sort of thing really made any positive contribution to a lad's character, and whether in time to come, when he had a road-manager and a fleet of buses to take him to and from his gigs, he would tell crowds of assembled pressmen about days like that one – and whether they would believe him if he did.

2

The Real World

In a posh West End bookshop, browsing politely
Coming upon a poem about orf
And feeling, as it were, betrayed by it.

Standing on golden carpet, smelling pus,
Feeling the rough scabs, touching the helpless
Sealed-together Papageno lips and wondering
How many of the people browsing here
Knew orf. Knew sturdy. Even suspected
The thousand-and-one named scourges of a world
I'd folded-up and left, thinking it safe
Till my eventual return to it.
Now here it was, and one of its sad facts
Held up for anyone to stare at it,
Take it at scar-face value from the book.

And then again
Perhaps it was the poet I'd betrayed
By knowing he spoke only shepherds' truth.
Even a stark tale of the taking of life
Is hardly news to the one random reader

Whose fingers bear the purple lambing-stains,
Who knows the sharp smell of the wet birth-coat,
Has groped in crowded wombs for gristly feet.
Was all this simply a coincidence?

And in a corner of the shop, I wept
Causing discomfiture among the staff.
Unsettling the other customers.
Snivelling for myself, and for the poetry—
Lying so long asleep in a closed book
Waiting a momentary congruence;
A single, sharp, exquisite relevance.

And still I kept on writing my regular, weekly column from the farm in the hills. Now and again people would ask me how I managed to do it, week after week, and at first I would grin inside and think to myself what a jolly good egg I was. So reliable. A brick – and a talented brick to boot. What I had not realized, except in a vaguely commercial sense, was how dependent I had become on there being someone there, week after week, to read it.

I had appreciated that the discipline of writing was one of the few strands that ran through the hazy days, taut and indisputable, like piano-wire, holding everything together. I had realized, too, though never allowing myself to dwell on it, that there was a sort of ongoing comfort in the sure and certain knowledge that any misery sooner or later became copy and was written, printed, shared, spiked.

The writing was a pleasure, the printing a compliment, the spiking inevitable and a good antidote to *hubris*, but I had not labelled the sharing; had hardly thought about it until I sat down to write my first letter to Leeds in the week after Andy went back to London.

Cheerily, as ever – 'it's real brass monkey weather up here, folks, lots of snow still lying over everything. . . .' Everywhere I went regularly – up the hill to feed the sheep, round the yard to feed the cow and the pigs – had become permanent pathways of polished ice and everything seemed to be hanging fire, waiting for it to melt. The road itself was no different. Due to some economies in public spending there had been no grit or salt spread in the interim, so that the great humps of solid ice still lay in the middle and the tracks that Boris made had become part of them.

The things we did that week in an effort to keep ourselves warm were an entertainment in themselves. There were blankets everywhere. I got a grim bank statement accompanied by a brightly coloured leaflet offering to help me 'cash-plan my holiday' and I didn't know whether to laugh or cry. I got a bag of coal from the village and it seemed to have been treated with fire retardant. I got hold of a couple of bags of 'compressed straw briquettes' which looked like donkey-droppings and burnt with great coils of volatile ash and no perceptible flame, like indoor fireworks.

I did drag a few beech trunks into the kitchen so that I could have a go at them with the little electric chain-saw, but they were as hard as concrete and all the damp sawdust from the attempt was trodden within hours all over the house, sticking to the damp floors and adding to the overall air of dereliction, and I didn't care. I gave up on it and concentrated all my attention on Henrietta.

Some time earlier, an undisciplined dog belonging to unexpected visitors had slipped out unobserved and made its way into the fold yard where my many hens scratched among the straw between the feet of Jim's cattle. It had caught and worried old Henrietta.

As a pullet, Henrietta had been found wandering all alone on the central reservation of the A19, and brought to me as a gift more years ago than most hen-memories are allowed to reach. She had twice appeared on television. She was loved and a bit special, and I had tried to nurse her as best I could. Now, though, I could smell gangrene in the ragged wounds on her breast and I should have resigned myself to giving up on her, too, but something was holding me back.

That winter had been a bad one for more reasons than the extreme weather, but there was a sort of comfort in my private misery. Fate, I told myself, had surely exhausted its ammunition. I resigned myself to parting with Henrietta; after all she'd had a bloody good innings and she was well past her prime. Like me. And then the phone rang.

Andy's voice, weak and frightened. 'Mum. I'm in hospital. I've had an operation. I wanted you to know.' All broken and incoherent as the trolley-phone swallowed his change and he muttered groggily between the stuttering pips until the greedy machine beat him and shrilled its triumphant monotone while I held it to my ear until my face ached, willing his voice back.

And there I was, penniless in the middle of nowhere, and there wasn't a damned thing I could do. And I found myself despising the busy caring I conveyed to my readers, week after week, and with it the overtones of jolly-hockey-sticks and never-say-die. And I hated the powerlessness and the poverty and the cold and even, in some strange way, the bundle of stinking feathers in the cardboard box at my feet.

But I made up my mind there and then that she would not die. Not if I could help it. I would give her penicillin and brandy and if she would not take them I would force-feed them to her. After all, they did similar things to geese in Strasbourg. I would nurse her to distraction and will her well as if in some way some of the loving and the caring would find its way out of that suffocating place and into the real world where it could do some real good to some real people. Perhaps.

And in a muddle of impotent rage and loneliness, I wrote it down. And what was supposed to be a jolly column, a celebration of life-on-a-shoestring and oneness-with-nature turned into a startling confession that there was no more gilt on the gingerbread and I was cold, tired and scared. And the thing that surprised me most was not that I had done such a thing, but how easy it had been.

A week later, with the inevitability of a long-standing promise, I sat down to write again. I had borrowed money, visited Andy and returned with a sense of real unease about his post-operative condition. He had only had his appendix removed, a straightforward run-of-the-mill procedure hardly more serious than basic bodily maintenance, but had one of my creatures seemed so strange or been running such a roaring temperature, I would have assumed something was very wrong.

I borrowed more money to visit again. Now the nurses, too, were worried and I asked to speak to the doctor who was in charge of Andy's treatment. He was young enough to be my son, too – and he called me 'mother', but in a tired, superior sort of way – 'It's natural for you to be worried, *mother*, but his temperature is within normal limits. Leave it to us. . . .' Andy was complaining about severe chest pain.

'Most post-operative patients suffer a bit of constipation – your son is just making a bit more fuss than usual. He'll be all right. . . .' But I knew he wasn't, and I persisted. I asked the doctor if he could convince me that Andy's temperature was not a sign of acute infection, and he sighed exaggeratedly before oozing condescension – 'It wouldn't be worth trying to explain, because the medical terms would only confuse you and worry you even more. . . .' I panicked.

But only for a moment. I suddenly thought of my sister's husband, who had recently been appointed clinical tutor at Addenbrooke's in Cambridge. 'If I asked someone with medical experience to enquire on my behalf, through hospital channels, would it make any difference?' 'No,' he said. But it did.

Back at the farm I rang Laurence. He agreed that the symptoms were alarming and said he'd see what he could find out. Within hours the consultant in charge of the doctor I'd spoken to was on the telephone asking if I could come back to the hospital. Andy was in no danger but there had been a mistake and they owed me an apology. I rang for a taxi.

The consultant, a tall, slim woman with an air of real authority as distinct from officiousness or bombast, met me in the ward sister's office. She showed me an X-ray. In Andy's abdomen was a huge abscess, so large it was forcing his diaphragm upwards, accounting for the severe pain. Andy had been operated on again and was now in intensive care. A room nearby had been put at my disposal.

'A junior member of my staff has made an error of judgement, for which I hold myself responsible. I offer you a sincere apology.' I accepted it, thanked her for taking my doubts seriously and for acting quickly. It wasn't until after

I lay down on the basic little bed in the noisy room where I would spend the next few days that the thought occurred to me – but if I hadn't had a brother-in-law in the trade – what then?

And while all this was going on, what of the farm? Nan and Robert kept it all going and I didn't think I'd been much missed until I read an essay that Nan wrote, detailing a day's work in my absence. It sounded like the testimony of a child labourer in some unenlightened Third World economy.

Speaking of which, the economics of those desperate weeks didn't bear thinking about. Fares to London were quite beyond the reality of my budget yet one of my children needed me and the money had to be found. On one of the early visits I asked to see the social worker at the hospital and she wrote a note to the local DHSS explaining the situation and asking them to issue me with a travel pass. I took it to the Benefits Office as soon as I got back.

The travel pass was a non-starter. I would have to give up the Family Income Supplement with which I was topping up what I could earn for myself and apply for Supplementary Benefit. Then, being in receipt of that, I would be eligible for assistance with travelling expenses to visit Andy. I agreed to this and the questions began. At 11.30 I left the office, walking on air. I was eligible for the assistance. I was to come back and pick up a counter giro at 2.30.

That was a wonderful three hours. I sat in the café, and wrote a couple of letters. I went to the bank, told them I'd be back with a giro cheque after lunch and they gave me money on the strength of it so that I could book my next trip south at the travel agent while I was waiting. I went to the taxi office, paid Marge for my last taxi and ordered my next one. And when I went back to the DHSS at 2.30 they had changed their minds.

They said it was because the twins, Robert and Nan, had passed their sixteenth birthday and the fact that they were still at school made no difference. The clerk who had seen me earlier told me that it was a hard and fast rule and that there was nothing they could do about it. Then she left me alone in the little hardboard cubicle coming tearfully to terms with the news.

Well, if I wasn't entitled, that was that – but why had they allowed me to believe, just for that tiny breathing space, that my troubles were over? I was trying to find a way to express how it felt, this sense of let-down, of misery, of helplessness in the face of authority. It had all been for nothing. The self-humbling, the pleading – the humiliation of hearing someone paraphrase what I had said and then read it back and hand it over for signature, like the police with a confessed criminal. I had only wanted their help for as long as Andy needed it and I had really believed for three weightless hours that I was going to get it. And now this feeling of – what?

I remembered just after the war, when sweets were hard to get, pretending to share a small piece of sticky chocolate with our dog. My mum was very cross, explaining that I should not raise false hopes in the poor old thing. 'Why?' I asked, although I expect I knew perfectly well even then. Mum answered me anyway, 'Because it's cruel,' she said.

Henrietta, who had been dying slowly of the effects of festering wounds on a very old bird eventually went back out-

side with her companions and although she was still unable
to flutter up to her perch, she would hop on to the warm
back of Charity the cow and spend her nights in solitary
state. She waddled too slowly to keep up with her scurry-
ing sisters but she could get about after a fashion though, a
week before, any effort to move would pitch her forward on
to her face where she waited for someone to come and pick
her up.

And someone always did, because she was my special
sacrifice. In the old days, when people wanted their god to
do them some special favour, they would kill something
and offer it up. I never saw the logic of that. Henrietta was
a sort of anti-sacrifice. It was as if I were offering up the sav-
ing of her in return for something I couldn't achieve for
myself; putting my caring and conscientiousness on some
private, personal altar in return for a little extra power to
expend on behalf of Andy, who seemed so very far away. I
suppose you could call it a kind of prayer.

That was how I tried to explain it to my sister on the telephone. I told her of the antibiotics I'd administered and the
hours I'd spent flicking grains of wheat one at a time on to
the back of her funny folding tongue so that she swallowed
them with a blink and a gulp. I described her poor bald
breast where I'd clipped all the feathers down to stubble to
get at her injuries and I made her laugh at my ham-fisted
attempts to suture the torn flesh – like darning a damp and
grubby vest; at my attempts to exercise her useless legs,
pedalling them for her as though she were riding upside-
down in the *Tour de France*; at the invention of a programme
of physiotherapy for her gnarled and skinny feet. And we
laughed far more than the jokes justified, because she
understood that I needed the relief.

It was only later that I realized that I needed her, too. I who had revelled in my glorious self-sufficiency – emotional if not financial – was grateful at last for the little sister who had brought her cuts and bruises and broken things to me a different life ago.

It was she and Laurence who had given me the book token that I took with me into Claude Gill's bookshop in Oxford Street next time I visited Andy and spent there on a collection of poetry – Ted Hughes's *Moortown* – because it made me feel I still existed.

3

Up the Wall

Something there is that doesn't love a wall. . . .

Mending Wall by Robert Frost

Something there may be; but it isn't me.

Any visitor to England's uplands will have remarked at some time on the dry-stone walls.

Some do so from the near-enough-to-touch viewpoint, stopping by the side of the road to size up the components and to convince themselves that they are nobody's and have as much right to continue their existence in a suburban rockery as to remain because 'after all, they're doing no good where they are'.

Others see them from moving cars, tutting at their dereliction. 'Why don't they put them up again when they fall down?' not realizing that they do, they do and they do.

Still others, nearer to the heart of the matter, take field-glasses and stare at the long lines of grey stones marching straight up hillsides, sometimes for miles, standing proud for just a split second before disappearing over far-off crests. Their reactions are manifold but somewhere in them all will feature the question 'Why on earth . . .?'

Why indeed. There are as many reasons as there are walls.

There is a right way to build them; Jim showed me. A double row of flat stones, back to back with their best faces outwards, the space in the middle filled in with all the small awkward bits that lie around. No pieces should be left in view because this looks slovenly. Every so often a long flat stone (a threeaf) will be made to lie from front to back. Ideally this stone will have two short smooth faces to present to the world and an even thickness so as to lie flat within the wall and tie the two sides together. Sometimes a really big threeaf will be put in two or three courses up from the ground and the stones below it removed to make a smout or thirl-hole. This will provide a way in and out for sheep and can be closed by rolling a round rock into it when expedient.

I spent many hours helping Jim to build these high-quality walls, doing the 'lad's job' of filling the middle. I spent many more though, throwing up what Jim called 'wonderwalls' – you wonder how long they can stay up – literally piling one stone on another, hardly pausing to select or amend, hardly even looking to see where each one sits before bending to haul up the next, tossing it as though it were red-hot, to clack into place alongside the last one. This is the method used for 'gapping-up' in a hurry and is the hill farmer's most often applied method, the showy stuff being saved for wet days in haytime and walls near the farm gate.

Gathering the moor two or three times a year sends a great woollen tide surging down from the high places and into the intakes between the moorland and the farm. Rarely will the gate suffice to admit them and they hurl themselves at the walls, leaping and scrambling up and over and inevitably sending them rumbling to the ground here and there in their enthusiasm for the rough grass beyond.

On a warm summer evening, as the tired ewes fill their bellies and the lambs bleat about as they match themselves each to an udder before nightfall, shadowy figures will move along the ravaged walls piling up the tumbled stones which need only to stand till morning and anything beyond's a bonus. The valley echoes to the random crack of stone on stone as the wonder-walls rise along with the first stars.

Stone walls, said Richard Lovelace, *do not a prison make*. He's right, but I wonder if he, too, came to that conclusion through livestock handling.

Probably not. I'm pretty certain that he was considering freedom of a more abstract nature and I tried to put his assertion out of my mind as I struggled, stone by massive stone, to create a wall along the front of the house that would enclose my yard and prevent all my four-legged dependents from having such direct access to my own living quarters.

Even the cow had been able to park and dump on my very step since the ravages of time and a spectacular gale had put paid to the post and rail fence that had guarded my castle, albeit half-heartedly, hitherto.

Ramshackle though it had been, when it was gone I missed it. Suddenly there was nothing between me and the livestock and old friends suddenly became adversaries who, now that my defences were breached, stood siege under my very walls. If I slipped out to go anywhere I was likely to be knocked down in the rush of assembled creatures trying to get in.

I thought about replacing the posts and rails but it would have been at best a bodged job and I thought about putting up a wire and stake fence but cash flow problems put a stop to that. There was no alternative; I would have to build a wall. After all, I had served my apprenticeship and done quite a lot of solo repair jobs here and there and they were none of them too bad.

I knew that, because every time I did a bit of walling I'd go round looking critically at every wall that crossed my path or ran parallel to it, mentally awarding points for technical merit until I had either found an acceptable number worse than mine or begun to take mine for granted. A wall it would be.

A wall, after all, has two undeniable advantages; all the materials are free and virtually indestructible, so that even if some accident should befall the structure the components will remain almost unscathed and all you have to do is pick them up and start again. So I started.

When the old buildings along the lane were demolished and made safe, the rubble was left where it lay. I had helped myself to the wieldier pieces to create a little paddock behind the house, but the biggest ones were still there, ideal for the footings of my new front wall. I borrowed a barrow.

The wall was three courses high and I felt like an elderly ape with my arms all stretched and dangling by my sides and my gait reduced to a shuffle because my thighs had heaved just too many mighty rocks for their own good. Slower and slower the job went and the assembled creatures watched my struggles, mentally noting the weak points for future reference. But it was a happy way to spend time, and to spend it as near home as I needed to be, it being spring and lambing looming.

I walled steadily away, one stone at a time, savouring the pleasure of anticipation, the new clement weather and the satisfaction of the job itself. I came out again after tea to do a bit more, working by now on instinct and determination, until it began to get dark.

I could see the stone I wanted. A sort of flat, solid-look-ing one of a nice even thickness. Just right for crossing the joint between the last two squarish, cobbly ones. I had nearly finished the section I was working on and it was coming to that point where the daylight decides to give in gracefully and you can really straighten up like a proper Yorkshire person and say 'It's about night'. I was trans-forming the available stones into a fairish approximation of a wall that would turn cattle if they didn't lean too hard and even turn the sheep while they were heavy in-lamb and dis-inclined for jumping.

Tired but pleased with myself I went to pick up my nice flat stone. I settled my feet at either side of it, took a good grip with both hands and lifted it swiftly. Far too swiftly. It flew up like a polystyrene boulder on a film set and I tot-tered backwards with the unexpected ease of achievement. In my hand I held the beautifully sculpted cardboard crust of a healthy pat of cow dung which had been crisped by the fine weather. It was a sure sign that it really was 'about night'.

I resisted the impulse to skim it like a frisbee down the hill for fear it should behave like the plastic ones that chil-dren play with and return on an elliptical course to hit me under the ear. Instead I took it into the house and set it on top of the sitting-room fire to see if the Punjabis had a wrinkle or two worth adopting. It burned better than I expected but smelled much as you might imagine it would while it was doing it. I'm not usually one to pass up an available resource but I decided not to repeat this experiment.

Mistakes with manure are a feature of our family history it seems. They tell a tale down in Steeple Bumpstead of the time my grandfather's cap blew off on just such a fine spring evening as he was coming home from the Green Man across the meadow among the grazing bullocks. They say he spent some time trying to decide which one it was before he could pick it up and put it on. Apocryphal no doubt, but feasible, as you would have been forced to admit if you had ever seen my Gramp's everyday cap.

Winston Churchill, I was once told, used to build walls by way of recreation and I wondered if he had ever had a similar experience but I don't suppose so, since he built with bricks and mortar and a brick is a brick is a brick and there's not much you can mistake it for except another brick. Poor Sir Winston missed out on the infinite variety of materials and methods and mental approaches available to the dry-stone waller.

Walling for the walling's sake can be a fine way to spend a day and there is satisfaction in the creativity of it, but when there is a gap that must be stopped in a hurry and all that you can find at the point of collapse are four or five mighty boulders and a handful of coarse aggregate then all you can work towards is that temporary triumph of mind over matter, a wonder-wall. Walling is a wonderful exercise in flexible goal-setting.

But the front wall was a set piece, done from scratch, and the evening was fine and fair. The wind blew strong and warm across the valley; nothing could diminish the feeling of freedom that comes from working outdoors without a coat on. To have the ground dry enough to go about in plimsolls was one of the sweet and simple pleasures that surprised me every year with their intensity. Like the twiddling of ungloved fingers in the early morning air, it was a giddying sensation of gaiety, all sharp and clean like the smells on the boisterous, friendly wind.

Outside my window, like a great cat asleep, lay the soft, gentle bulk of Sunburnt Nab. It forms the eastern end of the first fold of the Hambleton Hills; back to back with Black Hambleton, like distant book-ends, it stands guard over the untidy little valley of Upper Ryedale.

I had long ceased to be intimidated by its dominance and was comforted by the benign presence which became as familiar as the objects within the house and I spent much time watching the great soft slope as though it were the loved face of a treasured friend.

When we first came to Hagg House it was autumn and the softened sun painted the winding-down of the summer vegetation with every conceivable shade of honey and wine. After that I watched every change, from the melting of the last of each snow to the gathering greenness of twenty springs; from the slow brown deaths of bracken to the sudden comings-out of heather.

The odd thing was I hardly ever climbed the hill whose summit lay in a direct line from my front door and it remained always the sort of expedition that was planned and projected, talked of by visitors and then saved for future visits, as though it were an assault on the Eiger.

One summer I went up there in a state of mild confusion

which I felt would be helped by looking down on my world from the other side of the valley. It was there that I found the pile of stones scattered on a heathered outcrop just below the highest point of the hill. I remembered being shown how to find my way home from any point on the moor above my house – 'my' moor, where my own sheep ran. I was told to head directly for 'the stone man on Sunburnt Nab' and sure enough I had always been able to see the little stone cairn sticking up from the skyline like a pimple on a giant's bottom.

I was not conscious of its having disappeared; after all it wasn't exactly a dominating feature of the landscape. I just took it for granted that it was still there and I had long since become so familiar with my own stretch of moor that I had not had need to look for it. Now there it lay in ruins, and I took time to rebuild it roughly. It pleased me to see it once more on the skyline although it took a bit of spotting on a hazy day.

During the following winter, though, whether through the action of the wind or the over-enthusiastic rubbing of itchy sheep, it fell down again and I determined that one day I would make a special expedition to renew it properly. I would do it as an anonymous gift to the dale and to the people who had taught me the skills I needed to do it well.

And one day, about the time I realized that the only way to escape the unbearable changes that were killing me from within was to make some of my own before it was too late, I made the pilgrimage to restore the stone man. Down the fields, over the river and up, up, up I went until I was sitting high and mighty on the ridge of my small world's roof. Tractors moved in the fields like beetles on a carpet. My own house lay in wait for me halfway up the opposite hill.

In the field below it my solitary gander stood guard over a little black hen and her seven chicks, his whiteness showing up like a lost hanky in an asphalt playground.

I made a good job of that cairn, though I say it myself; the stones were carefully chosen, the middle meticulously filled. When I got back it was gloriously visible from my favourite seat beside the geraniums in the front yard. I preened a little, a latter-day Tutankhamun smugly observing his gift to posterity, or Ozymandias, perhaps, leering at his likeness in the desert. My friend Wendy, sitting beside me on the step, was gratifyingly impressed.

'However did you build that?' she asked. I began to explain. 'I just laid the first stone and then went round and round in ever-decreasing circles until. . . .' I caught her eye and grinned.

'Story of my life, really,' I said, and we went indoors for tea.

4

Dog Days

On reflection, perhaps the most important creature on the farm in those final years was Turpin, the sheepdog. He brought joy with him when he came.

The littlest, least promising pup of a litter born to a bitch I had, after a visit from a dog of Jim's, he somehow summed-up the philosophy of the farm: sell the perfect; keep the precious. When now and then I was tempted to lose sight of this, the first principle of peasantry, it was always some such chance-come-by or ill-begotten asset that reminded me of my promises.

He was born with no tail and no soft palate. From the start his front end sniffled and his rear end drooped. I carried him around in my pocket and fed him with a syringe and he grew into the best dog in the world.

He always looked somehow not-right, and he was never as clever as we pretended, but a whole family loved and protected him and he grew to fit the dog-shaped place in it perfectly.

Perhaps it was all that assiduous looking-after in his formative months that led him to become, in his turn, a committed and conscientious carer for anything that appeared in need. Rita Pig, farrowing for the first time, had reason to be grateful for this, but so far as I know she never was.

She too, was one of the ugly ones, kept back from a litter of better-favoured pigs which I sold in the summer. The following January she herself became a grunting, gloating mother with giggling, gurgling babies of her own, but the night that produced this triumphant first family also produced the following true though untidy tale with a most unlikely hero.

The first I knew of Rita's confinement was the sound of a pigfight from the sties. I went to see what was going on and saw Rita, knee-deep in snow, biting something I couldn't see. When she saw me she ran back into the sty.

I looked at the object lying in the snow. I thought it was a potato, but it was a piglet, almost frozen and bleeding from a nasty wound on its shoulder.

Inside the sty, Rita's little niece Shirley was poking happily at another piglet which lay in the straw. It squealed and Rita made a dive for it. I beat her to it and ran with the sorry pair into the house. I put them in a cardboard box in front of the electric fire in my bedroom and went back outside to give Rita the comfort and privacy that should have been ready for her and to fasten the inquisitive Shirley somewhere safely out of the way.

I settled Rita down and waited until the next piglet came. She grumbled a lot and I stroked her and talked to her but still when the newcomer arrived she got to her feet and barked irritably. Then it began to squeak and a great bubbling cry of rage burst from her and she made a grab for it. I scooped it up and ran with it, but this time Rita chased me, snapping, and I ran with the tiny wet pig like a determined rugby player diving for the line.

Back in the house I went to put this piglet with the other two, but one had climbed out of the box and was shivering under my bed while the other seemed to be at death's door. I moved the box nearer the fire, prayed it wouldn't catch alight and ran out again to try to fasten Rita into her nice warm sty and persuade her to settle to her work, but again when the piglet was born she was upset and angry.

It is a natural reaction for a sow with piglets to respond to their squeals, but the anger should be directed at whatever threatens them, not the youngsters themselves, although a gilt with her first litter can sometimes get confused, especially if her farrowing has been mismanaged like Rita's. I felt frightened, guilty and helpless. Nothing could be done now until the farrowing was over. Then I could give her a shot of tranquillizer and give her her babies back. Meanwhile, though, I had to rescue them as they arrived.

Back in the house with another, and all the rest had escaped again. They were cold and shivering round the skirting-boards. I spread a blanket in front of the fire, hoping they would stay where they could see the glow, but then I had to rush outside again as another murderous outburst from Rita meant another rescue was necessary. I felt horribly alone and heard myself whimpering, 'Oh, somebody *help*. . . .' as I dodged the snapping Rita and ran with another new-born to safety.

But this time all was peace in front of the fire; the little ones lay in a happy pile and the latest, moistest one was being licked lovingly by the strangest foster-parent. Turpin had taken over as crèche-master and looked hangdog at me as though he expected a reprimand, sure that such pleasure must be forbidden. I reassured him by patting his head perfunctorily and laying the new piglet between his paws – 'Good dog, oh *good* dog!' – before I ran out to save the next victim.

Nine piglets came, nine were saved and, after the farrowing was over, nine returned to their dopey, delighted mother, who crooned and burbled to them like any other sow with a new litter. But back in the house I sat on the crumpled blanket, speckled with bits of straw and smelling of pigs. Before me on the grate sat a steaming mug of tea and beside me sat the saviour of the situation. Turpin had watched over his little charges for nearly four hours, licking the wet and sticky ones and gently retrieving the older, bolder ones when they strayed too far from the warmth in search of food.

I hugged his big, stiff body and he licked me. 'Get off, pig-breath,' I said, but held him all the tighter. He licked again, quite at ease with my contradictions. 'What would I do without you?' I asked him. He just yawned and settled himself across my legs without bothering to reply. He knew, though. And so did I.

Tom was a large white rabbit, soft, droopy and portable; the sort of rabbit whose days are numbered in the free-and-easy country environment where the wild rabbits have eyes in their behinds and every dog is a hunter with *carte blanche* to kill, so long as it's rabbits he's after. Turpin had been known to lollop off after the odd indigenous bunny, but his attitude to Tom was different. Tom was family. Turpin could always be trusted to 'watch Tom' while he was out, and to 'fetch Tom' when it was time to put him in again.

'Fetching Tom' was perhaps the nearest Turpin ever got to a parlour trick. In response to the command he would whizz up to wherever the rabbit was cropping grass and seize him by the scruff. The fact that Tom never attempted to avoid capture seemed proof that he didn't mind this. Then Turpin would carry Tom home, walking stiff and holding his head up high. Tom, however, when held by the scruff, was longer than Turpin was tall and he would be returned to his hutch after a sort of white-knuckle ride, sometimes sledging on his back down the hill, sometimes semi-hopping on his hind legs to avoid having his dangling haunches bumped against the occasional obstacle.

One summer night we let Tom out for an hour before turning in and I ate my supper on the step, watching him lollop about. Oatcakes from the Scottish highlands and honey from Ithaca, gifts from friends returning from holidays. I swallowed the last of my tea (from Presto in Northallerton – some things one has to buy for oneself!) and then Turpin fetched Tom and we put him back in his hutch with a couple of oatcakes for later. Then I went to bed.

I was awoken suddenly by Turpin pawing awkwardly at my shoulder. There was a noise outside that I couldn't identify. I was aware that someone was in the yard. There was a crash, a pause – and then an eldritch shriek which sent me running to the back door. Tom! Something had got poor Tom.

Sure enough, when I ran out into the yard something was standing over Tom's outstretched body, from which rose the thin wail that serves rabbits for a swansong – 'I who am about to die. . . .' 'Shirley Pig!' I shouted, with an imperiousness entirely foreign to my nature, 'come here!' A large pink creature detached itself from the shadow under the wall where Tom's body lay limp and still and trotted over, wuffing cheerfully. She had escaped from her sty and, in search of pickings, had upended Tom's hutch and pinched his oatcakes. She had no evil designs on his person whatsoever; she was just searching for crumbs.

With Shirley safely back in her sty and Tom comforted as best we could, Turpin and I went indoors. Tom came too and I put him in a Famous Grouse box at the foot of the bed as he seemed to be still in a state of mild hysteria. At about four in the morning I woke suddenly and looked around. In the new, grey light I could see Turpin's ungainly form on the sheepskin beside the bed. I saw, too, the upturned box wherein I had put the rabbit. As my eyes adjusted slowly I made out the sprawled white form beside Turpin. They both twitched and shifted. Turpin sat up and looked at me.

'Whatever are you doing with that rabbit?' I asked him. 'Poor Tom's a'cold,' he replied, snuggled up to him and went back to sleep.

It was Queen Elizabeth I, so they say, who was so captivated with the exploits of Falstaff in Shakespeare's histories that she expressed a desire to see 'Sir John in love' and the bard obliged with *The Merry Wives of Windsor*. Turpin's love life, aside from the unswerving devotion he showed to me and to anything that he was asked to 'mind', was brief, but too important to go unrecorded. He showed interest in only one bitch, and that was a tiny terrier belonging to one of Nan's friends. She was clever, resourceful, even-tempered and had ears like a fruit-bat, for all of which attributes she was worth cherishing. He pursued her mercilessly, she submitting to a variety of imaginative clinches as the bemused dog, driven by an inexplicit imperative, tried to determine who should do what to whom. So unlikely did union appear that nobody took any real notice; both dogs seemed happy.

At last she took control of the situation and with Nature's own initiative jumped up on to the step outside the house. Turpin made a clumsy attempt to follow her and lo! – he was in.

I did what I could to help, but the ensuing tie with the pair on level ground and the little bitch scarcely able to take her weight on her front paws was probably what deterred Turpin from ever again proceeding beyond foreplay.

The little bitch stayed with us for her confinement, and on the morning of the sixth of June she began making preparations for whelping. She was clearly in control, as usual, so I left her to it, looking in from time to time to make sure she was coping.

It was a typewriting morning with a deadline to beat. I was up early, fed the creatures and then sat down with a mug of tea, strategically placed, as a result of years of warm and wet experience, at a point on my desk where the gradually extruding carriage would not nudge it into my lap. It was raining outside. I knew because Turpin came in dew-pearled like Pippa's hillside and with the soft hair on his ears crimped into ringlets, as sure a sign of rain as any of the trusted indicators of my childhood – the giant fir-cone from Shirley Woods, the seaweed from Brighton and the plaster donkey from Lord-knows-where, whose string tail changed from blue to pink according to the weather, though I could never remember which way was wet. He went outside again almost immediately, and when I went to refill my mug I could see him sitting halfway up the hill behind the house, watching Beezus.

Beezus was a fat and woolly gimmer of indeterminate

breeding whom I had bought the year before so that my niece Katy, who came to stay in springtime, could have a lamb to feed and hug, like the children in her Enid Blyton books. She was a very Enid Blyton sort of child was Katy, and used up adults' time and space in a way my own children never did. When she left, Beezus slipped into the same demanding role, never straying far from the house, and Turpin adopted her as his own, following her everywhere, singling her out from any group of lambs, playing with her mercilessly and licking her half to death. He pulled out great gobfuls of wool and she always had bald patches, yet she always chose, whenever possible, to share his company and she was the only sheep with which he allowed himself such liberties. When it became obvious that spring that she was to have a lamb of her own I worried lest the boisterous goings-on which had become so much part of her relationship with Turpin should harm her precious cargo.

I need not have worried. As her girth increased and her pace slowed, so Turpin's approach altered. He and Beezus were never far apart but there was no more galloping and wool-pulling. It was as if he watched over her as she grazed, as if she felt more secure in his presence. All in my imagination, probably, but I enjoyed the feeling. It's always good when those we love, love one another.

Beezus's lamb, when it came, was a piece of pure potluck. We had no idea which of the available tups had brought it about. I still couldn't swear to it, though I think it must have been a Swaledale. It was a fat and huggable little darling with a face the colour of bitter chocolate, probably destined to remain hornless by the feel of its little round skull. I wondered how Turpin would feel about it, since Beezus clearly adored it. I had a bad moment during its first few days when I saw Turpin lying half-way up the hill with the lamb between his front paws, so limp and lifeless that for a moment I hardly dared breathe. What had happened to it? Surely he hadn't killed it?

I called to him with a strange squeaky voice that would hardly crawl through my constricted throat. He got up and trotted down the hill. The lamb rolled over, shook its little head, got up and trotted after him – 'Where to now, uncle Turpin?' Beezus mumbled something unintelligible with her mouth full of grass and went on with her munching, unconcerned. She was clearly happy to trust her childhood friend with her most treasured possession.

Clearly? There I go again, making more than is proper out of these instances of animal behaviour. Mind you, I'm not the only one. Jim came by later that day to feed his cattle. He saw Turpin up the hill watching conscientiously over his beloved sheep. 'What's he up to?' he asked. 'Oh, he's just finding himself a job to do,' I replied. 'I should hope so too,' said Jim, 'and him with a wife and kids to support.'

It was true. His little terrier bitch had given birth to two fine strong pups, both white. One was marked with black and the other with golden brown. I called them Dylan and Donovan, it being D-day.

5

Going Solo

It is her music that I'll miss.
It's come to be her perfume in the house.

From *Solo* by Diana Hendry

There was a Meatloaf LP on the turntable upstairs and it was moving me to tears.

Up till then I would have said that the only heavy metal that had made itself part of my life was the old wide-mouth shovel I shifted shit with, but I found I was weeping when the fat fellow started banging on about sharing the future with a modern girl. A modern girl, you see, was very much on my mind as I listened to the sounds from upstairs. Not just the music but the whole symphony of moving things, packing things and throwing things away. It was loud, but it couldn't quite drown the sound of a chapter of my life coming to an end, though it was happening so very quietly that I had to strain my ears to catch the faint rustle of the turning page.

Nan was moving to a bedsit in Northallerton and starting at college on the following Monday.

It's funny how children become inextricably bound into their own special music so that when they leave they take it with them. When Andy left for London there was no more Bauhaus, no more Stranglers. Even when they turned up on the radio, they didn't feel the same any more, because of memory.

Sounds from upstairs have always symbolized the apartness which was a gift I gave my children. They had a room each upstairs and I converted a downstairs room into a study-bedroom for myself. Admission in all cases was by invitation.

One dark and stormy night at the end of a week of unremitting rain I lay awake listening to the sound of Queen from Robert's room immediately above. Our Bob was, at that time, besotted with Queen, and because I looked on them as one of the more honest bands of the period with real musical expertise, I had become quite a fan myself. *A Night at the Opera* was playing, not loud but insistent and I sang along silently in the dark.

Suddenly Robert's voice called 'Mum!' though the music continued unabated.

I waited. He called again 'Mum!'

'What?' I grunted testily. It had been a long day and I was tired.

'Mum, there's a huge black bird just flown in my window.'

'It's probably a raven,' I said. 'I expect God wants us to build an ark.'

'Seriously, Mum, what should I do about it?'

'Tell him I refuse to make a start before morning,' I said,

pulling the quilt up round my ears while upstairs 'The Prophet's Song,' began:

O, O, People of the earth. Listen to the warning, the seer he said: Beware the storm that gathers here. . . .

I heard scuffling and the sound of bare feet on the landing.

I dreamed I saw on the moonlit stair. . . .

and then there was a knock at the door. I grunted. Robert pushed it open with his elbows and held out at arms' length a large droopy-looking bird. I admit I had half-thought he was joking. He opened his mouth to ask another question which turned to a shriek as the bird made a noisy bid for freedom, beating its wings furiously. For a moment Robert stood there like a knight of the round table with a hawk on his fist and then the bird flew – not up to the ceiling but down to the floor, and scuttled under my bed. The next thing I knew Robert was crawling under after it. By now I was wide awake.

O, O, Children of the land. Quicken to the new life. Take my hand. . . .

Robert let out a great shriek; 'The bastard bit me!' and scrabbled out arse first, looking woebegone.

Fly and find the new green bough. . . .

The bird skimmed across the room to perch on the

wardrobe, scattering papers from my desk. Robert made another grab and missed as the vicious beak sliced at his hand again. I told him to go and get my bale-stacking gloves from the kitchen dresser.

Return like the white dove. . . .

In he came again.

Late, too late all the wretches run . . .

and there began a comic chase of Looney Tunes proportions until I begged him to stop.

From mother's love is the son estranged. . . .

I told him to sit quietly for a moment while the poor bird calmed down. Upstairs Queen played on. Now it was 'Love of My Life.'

Bring it back, bring it back, don't take it away from me . . .

and gentler now he stalked the bird while I saved my energy to pounce on it, trying to keep a straight face as he spindled round the bedroom like an inept Apache. Queen were well into *Bohemian Rhapsody* by the time we finally got hold of it and I looked hard at it in the light of the bedside lamp.

It was an extraordinary thing, like no bird I recognized, with great dangling legs and skinny feet which, like the long, fierce beak seemed quite out of proportion with the slim athletic body. It was no crow, and far too big for a blackbird. It looked almost like a wader with those great feet. It gave a determined flutter and I tightened my grip around its shoulders as Queen sang:

Bismillah! No! We will not let you go!

and then Robert and I collapsed in a heap and laughed till we were drumming our heels on the carpet.

The bird spent the night in the bathroom. In the morning the storm had abated. I got out my books, identified it as a juvenile moorhen and let it go, watching as it flew straight and true down to the river. And when Robert left in the autumn to go to college in York, he took Queen away with him.

And now Meatloaf agonized to the thrum of a hundred Harley Davidsons and Nan poked her head round the door to ask if she might take one or two small things which were not strictly hers but part of her growing-up; part of home. I remembered going to pick up the reduced and tearful Andy after his spell in hospital and seeing his digs in Hackney where here and there were tins, boxes, bits and pieces of what had been common property that he had begged and brought away. I had never given their going a second thought until I saw them again there, in a new place. I was moved and flattered by his having wanted to take them, by what the taking told me. But I didn't say anything.

Nor did I say much to Nan, apart from 'yes' to most of her requests. She was looking forward to her new single selfhood but was finding the going hard. Sharply, brightly we talked to each other. She brought me a handful of tapes she had borrowed when she and her friends were going through a 'sixties' phase and I realized that from then on the only music in the house would be mine.

Music to complement moods, manic, angry, sad – music to write with, to create and remember with. Classical mostly, with here and there a pop song that mattered. I put one of the Beatles' tapes in the cassette player, softly so as not to compete with Meatloaf. At the end of side one I chose to rewind it rather than turn it over; side two begins with 'She's Leaving Home'.

Night was falling on the Drysdale farmlet; another long day was at an end. The pet lambs had given up wailing for the milk I could no longer afford to give them and had grudgingly eaten their weaner pellets instead. The pigs had been out for their evening wallow in the mud-hole and were back snoring in their sties with pink snouts hanging over the step so as not to miss anything. Turpin had wangled himself on to the armchair and lay folded up like a Swiss army knife. Peace reigned.

It had been a long day. Longer and more tiring than the days when I'd been a fancy-free farmer with a handful of grubby kids and at the ragged ends of days like that one I liked to sit and dream about how it all used to be.

Sort of rocking-chair-on-the-veranda syndrome, I now realize. At the time such dreams served to reinforce the conviction that it was worthwhile doing anything I could to hold on to it.

Jim often used to say, quoting some probably mythical forebear; 'If things don't alter, they'll stop as they are,' and at first I thought I understood, but when I took the idea home and looked at it critically, I saw that it said different things according to what mood you were in when you unwrapped it. Was it a magic formula for preventing change, an exhortation to preserve life-as-we-know-it by obsessive routine, or an admonition to the effect that if we do not allow progress we will invite stagnation? I muttered it like a mantra because it served to support my decisions in matters of importance whichever way you looked at it.

Now I was using it to justify a big step I had just taken, by telling myself it was a way of staying where I was. The rent had been quadrupled by a new Estate policy, the price of livestock had fallen and the cost of feed gone up. I was finding the growing financial demands of the farm impossible to sustain, so I had got myself a job. Not an exciting, sit-at-home, creating a masterpiece type of job. An ordinary, everyday, paying-the-rent kind of job. I was working part-time in an electrical shop. My uniform hung on the wardrobe door alongside the filthy wellingtons I had forgotten to take off outside when I came back from putting the pigs to bed. It was beginning to feel as though there were two of me and I was often unsure which of me I was.

Transport was as much of a problem as ever, but I coped by pedalling down to the village on my bike, catching the bus into Northallerton, doing my stint among the washing-machines and hi-fis and then getting the bus back to the village, fishing out my bike from my friend's shed and pedalling (and pushing) my way back to the hills. I worked it out that I cycled a half-marathon every time and was disappointed that I did not look fitter for it. I had it all worked out like a military campaign and would set off in farming gear with my uniform in the saddle-bag, stopping on the way to feed sheep, inject sick lambs and generally make sure all the outlying stock were coping before remounting my metal steed and heading west.

In no time the sheep had learned to gather at the moor gate at the sound of my Mickey Mouse bicycle bell and when I stood among them with the boldest ones shoving against my legs and the lambs bobbing about among them like children in a check-out queue I could hardly believe that I would soon be whizzing off up the silver ribbon road that dribbled like a small trail into the distance over the misty moor. I wondered whether my woollen friends watched the bright dot of my orange waterproof till it faded from sight like the last vestiges of a switched-off television picture. Or did I somehow cease to exist for them the way they did for me while I was in a world so very different from the one we shared.

For different it was; a great Aladdin's cave of consumer semi-durables with which I could hardly claim to feel at ease. I discovered that there is a world of difference between serving and selling; the first I enjoyed but the second frightened and slightly disgusted me, despite having been sent to Harrogate on a special course to show me how to do it. I scored highly in all aspects of the course except 'personal appearance'. They should have paid more attention to that, and so should I. I enjoyed putting a plug on a kettle for a lady who lived alone but felt uncomfortable selling a teletext colour receiver to a well-heeled gentleman. I was desperately deficient in what the management called 'product knowledge' since my life style had not led to familiarity with life's larger luxuries. But I tried, and I was grateful to the company for giving me the chance. And I learned a lot.

I learned the difference between features and benefits. I learned that a half load and an economy wash are not the

same thing. I found out which electric shavers had a mous-
tache-trimming attachment as standard and which did not.
I discovered what a camcorder was and soon knew enough
about joy-stick interfaces to pass queries on to somebody
more computer-literate.

But sometimes it was hard. Hard pedalling along into a
head wind. Hard getting soaked in the more-often-than-not
rain. Hard being abused on the telephone for a mistake in
somebody's account that had nothing to do with me. And
hardest of all sometimes just not being at home on a fine
sunny day when dust motes were spinning in the shafts of
golden light that filtered in from the outside world that was
still, for me, the only real one. I felt as though I were peeping out at it from the inside of a bottle. Now and then,
though, I would have to go for change to the shop next door
where sat, on a shelf, copies of my last two books with faces
of my beloved creatures looking down at me and I told
myself that there were worse things to sell one's hippy soul
for than a continuing supply of pigfeed.

One happy morning Rita Pig, now a portly matron,
delivered herself of a dozen youngsters and although my
presence was in no way necessary to the success of the venture, she was good enough to allow me to share in the
warm and busy goings-on that ended so satisfactorily. No
gritted teeth, no toil and travail, just a long sighing semi-
sleep that was punctuated now and then by the easy arrival
of intermittent little pigs, slipping like slivers of wet soap
from a clenched fist. A wriggle, a sneeze and a slightly
unsteady journey under Rita's uplifted hind leg to the nearest place at table with all the exaggerated care that an ine-
briate takes on a necessary journey to the tavern toilet.

What a delight are tiny pigs! Rose-petal pink they are,

with a fine silvery down that trembles in their siblings' gusty breathing when they lie in a heap. When they arrive their ears are all packed flat for storage and their trotters are soft and chewy. They dry up and fill out like dragonflies in the sunshine till by the end of their first day they are pink and piggy, firm and fuzzy and quite obviously all set to seize life by the sharp end and live it to the full.

I knew all this; I had seen it all so many times before, but still I loved to share those first few moments when they spilled out like evacuees from a train, taking it for granted that they would be fed, that they will be welcome, wanted, loved. Only innocence takes such luxuries on trust.

Some of Rita's pigs had spots. Not many of them and not many spots either. At first I was delighted but then a thought crossed my mind that maybe it was not such a good idea. You see, a pig with a round black spot on its bottom is so very different from one who is spotless, as it were. It is a first step to becoming special, and so to becoming vulnerable. Little pigs, during their first few days, are subject to all sorts of disasters. They can be starved, stepped on, suffocated by their mother or their brethren, they can wander from the nest and die of cold – they can be snuffed out like little candles by any one of the thousand natural shocks that pork is heir to.

It was for this reason that I tried, wherever possible, to avoid loving any particular piglet too hard for the first few days, just in case. It lessened the pain of the occasional unavoidable accident.

Once those first, vital few days were over, though, I quite often gave the little ones names, especially as their personalities developed and they began to display the small differences that made each one special. But I found, too, that I often coped with life by playing it out at second hand through my pigs. They became people in the way dolls and bears do for children and I named them accordingly.

Rita was Rita because of a dear lady who was kind to me at a time when I was unhappier than ever before or since. Shirley was Shirley because of a joke I shared with someone who tired of the sharing before I tired of the pig. Diana and Susan and John all had reasons over and above their pigness.

The day after Rita's joyous confinement I went back to my job in the shop only to find that the powers-that-be had exchanged one of our trainee managers for another from a different branch and it was like awakening to one of the plagues of Egypt. Given the choice, though, I'd rather have had the frogs. I was told that I would learn a lot from him, and so it proved. I was not at all surprised that this young man was a consistent achiever of objectives, a constant surpasser of targets. He had what it takes to succeed in sales.

Coming home, I went first to see the new pigs and sat and watched them for a while. I looked for the spotty ones. They were all still there. The one with the big patch on his hip was up front again. One of the last to be born, this big strong fellow worked his way in a matter of minutes to the front teats – the ones that yield the most milk. Time and time again I moved him further back to give the little ones a chance but he always fought his way up again, knocking his smaller siblings unceremoniously aside. I thought of what I had learned from the new salesman.

I didn't move the big piglet again. I gave in. I accepted the fact that he was no team player, that he would always be on top. I tweaked his string tail. 'Hello, Eddie,' I said to him.

*

Soon after that I was taken into the staff room and shown the sales targets. I was well short of mine. I was told that I'd have to do better or they would have to 'let me go'. I went.

I had learned a lot and earned enough to buy a second-hand moped which eased the transport problems, but what I really needed was a job I could do from home. Telephone sales sounded feasible, because the person I was selling to wouldn't know whether or not I was executively dressed or if I smelled of pigshit. I saw an advertisement for people to sell natural phosphate fertilizers to farmers and applied.

I was invited to another training course in Harrogate. It started with a plenary session in which we were told that fewer than one in three of us would make the grade. Then we split into groups for intensive training. My group was taught by a bright young thing who used methods involving role-play and imaginary telephones. She referred to our archetypal customer as 'Mr Farmer' and regaled us with girlish giggles at his funny ways.

She told us among other things that the time to 'catch' Mr Farmer was at lunchtime – 'or dinner-time as he calls it' (giggle) – 'or at teatime when he comes in from the fields.' That, I thought to myself, is how to make yourself really unpopular with Mr Farmer, though I kept stumm, supposing she knew best. It was clear that the young lady didn't have too high an opinion of the intellect of her prey.

When it came to 'any questions' time, I asked what I should say when I was extolling the virtues of their super-product with added magnesium which she had told me was designed to combat 'grass staggers' (giggle). I knew a lot more about grass staggers than she did. I knew, for example, that livestock in areas prone to staggers would most likely be given magnesium supplements in-feed. What should I say to Mr Farmer when he asked me about the possibility of overdose?

She didn't know and said she had never been asked that question before but she would ask the managing director when we broke for lunch. She must have said something because he asked me to sit next to him, and we conversed throughout the meal. I tried all the sales tricks I'd learnt from the electrical retailers – listening hard to pick up his unstated needs and presenting my features so that they appeared as benefits – after all, I was selling myself to him. I soon learned that his great hero was Oliver Cromwell. I saw a glazed look pass across the face of the bright young thing and gathered that most of his staff were long since bored to tears with Old Noll. I put into practice all that I had learned from ever-ready Eddie and drew out from the dusty cupboards of my general knowledge enough about the Parliamentary cause to keep him happily expounding thereon until dessert. In the post the next day was a letter telling me that I was one of the chosen few, together with a list of local farmers who had been picked as likely targets.

Many of them were men I knew by sight from sheep sales, auctions and funerals. I decided to start with Mr C from Bilsdale. He said, 'Allo.' I swallowed and started. He said, 'Fuck off', so I did.

The following day I sent a letter to the managing director of the fertilizer company which began; 'I beseech you, in the bowels of Christ, think it possible you may be mistaken.'

6
The Shiny-shoe Boys

Strange fits of passion have I known
And I will dare to tell . . .

William Wordsworth

Not unsurprisingly, most of the men I met were farmers,
but there were a few who looked in from other worlds, like
aliens. Jim called them shiny-shoe boys. It was a derogatory
term.

Once upon a time the best café, in the western world was
the Odana, opposite the bus station in Northallerton. It was
frequented on a regular basis by the classes of people often
excluded from more orthodox establishments. There were
always motorcycles outside and a lot of black leather within.
Working clothes were almost *de rigueur;* pieces of plaster and
failed pop-rivets dropped like dandruff from dusty overalls
on to the vinyl tiles and were swept up discreetly later.
People from the sheltered workshops were welcomed by
name and their idiosyncrasies were never mocked or at least
never more than once. Fat Frank saw to that.

The food was simple. There was no *spécialité de la maison* – the cuisine was adapted to the customer in that anyone who came regularly to the café and usually ordered the same thing would have it automatically tailored to their taste. I hate the café fashion for mashing up hard-boiled egg with cheap mayonnaise before putting it in sandwiches; it makes the egg go further but the cloying sweetness is faintly disgusting. I don't like onions which seem always to lurk in café salad. Fat Frank would create my dream sandwich for me: crisp lettuce, tasty tomato, sweet cucumber and egg in slices, flat and round and white and yellow like simplified daisies. This was between two slices of fresh, white bread although most of his clientèle preferred onions and mayonnaise and flat, sad baps.

When he heard the sewing-machine sound of the little Honda outside the window he would pour tea as I preferred it, medium brown with milk and no sugar, and it would be on the table when I came in. Often he would join me and share his Mirror crossword, half-squatting in the aisle first, then shuffling up alongside. We became unlikely friends.

Fat Frank lived in a time-warp. The juke-box in the corner played mainly sixties' tunes. The special sandwiches and the double breakfasts served twelve at a time to shifts of builders and the single frothy coffees served to slow-sipping signers-on were consumed to the accompaniment of Bob Dylan, The Byrds, Moody Blues and Tommy Roe. And I, despite a preference for the classics, grew to love many of the songs I'd shrugged off the first time around.

The grim, glass-fronted greasy spoon was then as far from home as I needed to go to feel part of that other world where my children were starting to explore and grow, like hoggs sent down-country for the winter. Nan's first job was behind the hissing espresso machine on Saturdays. It was a link in the chain that was being slowly paid out between us.

The Odana, in Fat Frank's day, was simply a good place to be. I even wrote some of my articles on its Formica table-tops, pretending to be Maupassant.

Fat Frank, like Fat Freddy, had a cat. Kitty was his pride and joy. She was black and half siamese and came and went through a back window in his flat above the café. She being beautiful and the world being what it is, she produced several kittens before Frank got round to having her spayed. In one litter was an exquisite, tiny tabby and when I pointed out to Frank how very beautiful it was, he gave it to me.

It was female. She grew into the perfect short-haired mackerel tabby that is the very essence of catness. You know the kind I mean; a soft dun-colour with stripes that look as though they have been put on with Indian ink and a camel hair brush – laid on freehand by an expert, like coachlines on a vintage car, in a sort of defiant symmetry. On her forehead, between the eyes, a slick, black 'M', mysterious, somehow enhanced her charm.

I called her Mrs Willoughby, after a woman I knew only as a fleeting visitor to the electrical shop where I worked for a while. She was about my age, not pretty, but with that rare combination of classic elegance and unforced charm that are the stock in trade of a real lady.

One day the young manager was in some distress. He had hurt his back and was shuffling round the shop doubled up with agony. I fetched him pain-killers and made him cups of tea. I did his share of the dusting and fetched his take-away lunch. Then, half-way through the afternoon, the original Mrs Willoughby came into the shop. All the young men stepped forward but the manager swooped majestically from his bed of pain in the staff room and beat them all to the most obsequious 'may I help you?' that I ever hope to hear. Not only did he sell her a video-recorder, he carried it out to her car. Such is the power of true femininity. I called my little cat after her, not in spite – for she was a delightful woman – but more in a sort of wry envy.

I had another old cat at the time, who became Mrs Willoughby's benevolent mentor. Eric was the largest cat I had ever owned and seemed to go on growing till the day he died. He was a cheerful ginger with a bit flat face and a permanent feeble grin. He had a barrel body, great clumsy feet and a rather unsavoury rear view. People always compared him with dainty little Mrs Willoughby and treated him like the amiable clown he appeared to be. People openly pointed out his lack of feline grace. But sometimes, when I looked in the mirror, I had thoughts that were best left unspoken and then it comforted me to stroke my big, silly cat and scratch his odd little ears which stuck out sideways like knots in a hanky.

What seems now no more than an interesting incident was, at the time, an unexpected explosion of joy and despair. In the making of one of my television appearances I met a producer. He came to visit the farm with one of the pert researchers I had come to take for granted and seemed enchanted by my way of life. After the interview he kissed me a little longer and a bit harder than I had come to expect and said that he would see me soon. Letters came often and so, less often, did he. He had an ancient Vauxhall Victor and drove from Leeds bringing wine and flowers. It was summer and I convinced myself the relationship would fit comfortably around my farm and my family which was as yet unthreatened by more serious change. He said he loved me.

But it was over by the end of the summer. He had become an Executive and I had no idea what that was. He moved to Sheffield, started breaking dates and promises and exchanged the Victor for a brand new Sierra. He had to go to Brighton on business – arranging a reception on behalf of the TV company at the Tory party conference – and he had asked me to go with him, but before I had even got properly started on panicking about what to wear or what to tell the children, he wrote to say the arrangement was off.

I still have the letter. It still doesn't make sense, being couched in that extraordinary non-language, the flannel in which bad liars wrap lame excuses. I remember he used the phrase 'all that Heaven allows' and I wished he'd found a less faded quotation. I cried a lot and slept erratically. I was lying awake listening to the World Service when I heard the first report of the IRA bomb in the hotel where I was snivelling to be.

Terror turned instantly to action. I pulled on clothes, thrust bare feet into wellington boots and ran, shaking and gasping to the telephone box across the bottom of the moor. Cathy Earnshaw never fled over blusterous heather to her Heathcliff in such mindless haste, talking, praying, begging favours of the mean little wind that snatched what spare breath I had left.

He was all right. And, eventually, so was I. I have wondered since whether the thing began with some sort of bet. I heard recently that he has retired and settled abroad with a

woman whose name I heard once when he answered the
car-phone in the brand new Sierra. I hope they're happy. It
would never have been a go anyway. As Jim said acidly; 'He
never cuddled you after a day's dodding when you were all
sheep shit.' Neither he did. And when I learned only the
other day that the loveliest of his quotations, the only one I
couldn't place at the time, came from the soundtrack of *Lady
and the Tramp*, I'm glad I never gave him the chance.

I seldom succumb to the blandishments of the advertiser
who is more often than not as skilled at stretching and spinning as the deftest spaghetti twirler, although he manipu-
lates truth rather than paste. Nevertheless I did treat myself
to a Supermop because I believed, in a moment of unaccustomed naïvety, that it really would mop floors better than
the old sort.

Like most such things it proved a great disappointment
to me, having been designed for the Other Woman. She
who had a microwave and took it for granted. She who
could hang out her whites without shame. She who
referred to her bog-roll as bathroom tissue. She who had a
centrally-heated house with flat vinyl floors.

In my hands the Supermop was a mere fistful of flat
string. It shredded to pieces on the cement floor in the
kichen and the round thing in the middle screeched on the
quarry tiles in the living room like chalk on a blackboard. I
relegated it to the cupboard and resigned myself once more
to the occasional weary genuflexion with a washing-up
bowl and a worn-out vest. This, though, was the very
image I was trying to leave behind when I got the mop out
again and pressed it into service as a stiff and unprotesting
partner with which to practise the social foxtrot.

The first thing I found was that I couldn't take so much as a step while wearing jeans; not, that is, when called upon by the instruction manual to do everything backwards, which is what being female means in a ballroom. It's the same sort of feeling that still comes over me when taken short at a formal gathering – I cannot pee while wearing a hat.

I pushed the furniture back to the edges of the carpet and dressed myself in my best approximation to the yards of tulle that real dancers wear, upgraded by my imagination from an Indian cotton skirt that I bought for a pound in a charity shop because the colours in it reminded me of so-sorry winter skies.

A sorry sight we were, too, my Supermop and I as we tottered backwards by the book. 'Step back with the right foot.' With you so far, nameless instructor; now what? 'Step back with the left foot.' OK – but how far? Back as far as the right one? Or beyond? – and suddenly I was only ungainly Annie, standing on one leg while the world whirled by knowing exactly what it was doing and the music went on without me.

Oh, the music, the music! A borrowed tape of old standards. Victor Sylvester. Ambrose. All the sounds of the childhood of the lucky little girl whose Dad taught ballroom dancing at the Streatham Locarno. The little girl who tried so hard to learn the quickstep and thought she was making him cross when really she was making him sad. How he must have longed for a little girl with poise and patent shoes who could knock 'em dead in junior competitions.

Do it for Dad, then. Slow, slow, quick-quick slow and the sound of the words filled my head even though there were no vocals on the tape so that I was dancing alone under a Blue Moon. For me the magic of those old songs lay in the lyrics because that was the part that meant most to the little bookworm with the two left feet, and as I fidgeted round the floor with my mop they sang themselves in my head.

The mooted possibility of the Rockies tumbling or Gibraltar crumbling seemed somehow much more likely than that I should ever master the social foxtrot. But I persevered, tackling the problems at an intellectual level as they arose.

How far back should that left foot step? As far as the right or beyond? It seemed to me that the matter would be resolved under field conditions by watching carefully where my partner needed to put his own foot. If I didn't move mine far enough he'd tread on it; if I moved it too far he'd lurch forward and bite my tit.

And that was when I ended the association. I ran forward with perfect grace and gathering speed out of the kitchen door and into the moonlit yard. A javelin thrower, I tensed my biceps, drew my arm back and hurled that wretched Supermop as far as ever I could make it go. End over end it flew, its silly hair flopping now above, now below its one red, stiff leg. I heard the hiss as it buried itself in the nettles beyond the orchard.

The silence and finality somehow satisfied me. The Supermop had done no such thing. Not only was it no great shakes at shifting the dirt off my quarry tiles, it also made a singularly unresponsive dancing partner.

I had met Sebastian in the house of acquaintances in Osmotherley. I think they were matchmaking, or perhaps it was another bet and best not looked into. They said we had lots in common, but at the end of the evening I wasn't so sure. I ended the evening with a headache, remembering the fellow only as a maroon blazer and an orchestrated laugh and a recurring desire to kick myself for having said at one point 'Debussy' when it should have been 'Ravel'. It came as a great surprise when he invited me to be his guest at one of North Yorkshire's historic occasions – the last-ever dance at the Spa Pavilion in Whitby, which was due to be demolished.

That was how I came to be practising with the Supermop. When I finally wrote to Sebastian asking to be excused because of not being able to dance, he treated me to three lessons with a formidable lady called Janet Frowen who turned herself into a prince and my plimsolls into court shoes for an hour at a time under a dangling sphere of tiny mirrors that hung off-centre in the ceiling of her draughty premises, contradicting itself by turns; now chic, now kitsch. I couldn't decide whether it was really spinning or if it was an illusion, part of the fairy tale of here-today-gone-tomorrow that the Big Dance promises.

Cinderella did go to the ball. Mind you it took her all her courage and there were a lot of inhibitions to leave behind and a lot of fears to overcome. You see I was never one of the youngsters who gathered at a local palais. I never danced with a crowd of other girls around a central pile of handbags or adjourned to discuss the opposition in the powder room. I was under no illusions, knowing full well that it all had to do with the way of a man with a maid, but I disguised fear as disdain. I had never been told that dancing was lewd or undignified but somehow I felt inside myself that it was. That was an excuse, of course, a defence dreamed up at an age when grammar school girls were made to dance *à la Grecque* in dusty gym knickers and bare feet – and Isadora Duncan I was not.

As I grew older the problems got worse. What appears as a delicious coltishness in a young girl and an attractive gaucherie in a teenager is hopelessly unbecoming to a middle-aged mother. The last dance at the Spa was as important to me as a last tango in Paris and I took my preparation seriously.

It was a warm night. The sea was an insistent susurrus somewhere below the lights of the promenade while above them the tired old Spa waited for the last long line of dancers to effect their entrances widdershins through its idiosyncratic revolving door. There was no spinning ball on the ceiling, which was underdrawn with swagged curtains, yellow and white, like the chrysanthemums in Milne's poem about the displaced dormouse. I, too, was out of my preferred element, but still somehow I managed to have the sort of evening I missed out on when I was seventeen or so.

It wasn't only the comfortable undemanding Spa with its skid pan floor and erratic amplifiers that made it possible. There were echoes of Mrs Frowen: 'step, together, side, close.' Echoes of my father's 78s with the sound of wire brush on snare drum insisting the rhythm. Smiles of encouragement from Sebastian's teacher, who was clearly proud of him. An entertaining companion. A gentle and uncritical partner. All these things came together and formed themselves into something every bit as magic as the mirror moon that wasn't there, so that I, who had felt myself cast for ever as principal boy in life's pantomime at last found out what it felt like to play the princess.

So my farewell to the Spa wasn't quite so sad as it might have been. Ours was not a long acquaintance and, on an entirely selfish level, it seemed almost fitting that the place should now simply cease to exist like a plate broken on purpose in a Greek restaurant after an especially memorable meal.

7

The Ash Crook

It was a well-wrought thing; I cherished it.
One day I was careless and the old black sheep
Found it and naggled off great strips of bark
And ruined it. I mourned it for a day,
Then shrugged it off and made the best of it.
A working stick.
I sent the dog with it, caught lambs in the crook of it,
Leant into fierce winds on the strength of it.

It was one of the few things I brought away;
Not that it was costly or beautiful
But because I still like to walk with it
And feel the teethmarks of a good old friend.

Snuff and Lamb Chop. Ridiculous names from the begin-
nings of the farm, given – by accident and other people – to
two pet lambs who, between them, taught me about almost
every sad and messy disease small sheep can suffer from.
Snuff was an hour old when she came, coal-black, still wet,
in a cardboard box. She was a grown ewe with lambs of her

own when Lamb Chop joined us – a present from a well-meaning hippy who realized that keeping a lamb for ever between two fireguards in a layby was not really a go. Both became too precious ever to part with and they were among the few to whom I ever promised a home for life.

Snuff was a Suffolk cross. During her lambhood she lost the sight of one eye and always went about with her head on one side to maximize her field of vision. By the time she was two her neck was permanently twisted. She was small and ugly; a black bullet head with ears like knots in a hanky; a grubby-grey fleece on thin liquorice legs. She grew up with the children. I have a photograph of her wearing a panama hat; one of her wearing a gas mask. Nothing ever fazed her. Year after year she produced fine strong lambs and reared them lavishly. Pound for pound she was the biggest money-spinner on the farm.

Lamb Chop on the other hand was financial disaster from the beginning. An ill-favoured Swaledale with too-wide horns and a too-grey face, she lost several of her own lambs through ineptitude at the time of their delivery. It always took her at least forty-eight hours to acknowledge the fact that she had lambed at all. Many of those she did rear were remarkably unlucky, continuing my education in the giddy gallimaufry of methods by which sheep may die. Cerebro-cortical necrosis for instance. And listeria.

When the two old ewes were past their best but still had most of their teeth I had them fitted with metal braces so as to prolong their grazing life. Snuff's worked well and she kept it till the end, flashing a startling metal grin at visitors, but Lamb Chop's worked loose and dropped out a year or two later. When I next clipped her I helped the last remaining loose teeth from her gums – a ewe with no teeth at all

can manage to feed far better than if she still has one or two
– and since the rough heather and bilberry wires were now
too much for her, she was pensioned off from the moor,
declared an 'inside sheep' and came to join Snuff in the
fields round the house, an arrangement that suited her perfectly.

One Monday morning at the end of March I awoke to a
goodly covering of snow. The wind was strong, gusting
from the south-west, and there was a sizeable drift at the
back door. I went straight up to the moor to fetch the sheep
down and the blizzard up there was a hundred times
worse, blinding, soaking and freezing me. Luckily the
sheep were not far away and I soon had them safe in a sheltered field.

When I turned for home the wind had obscured my
tracks and it was strengthening and changing direction,
slipping inexorably round to the north east – the worst of
all possible winds.

Half way through cooking lunch the electricity supply
failed. At about half past one the telephone died with a
soulful clink and at half past three I decided that Lamb
Chop, who had been trying to lamb for an hour or two,
could probably do with a bit of help. With the blizzard
howling outside, I knelt in the barn beside her, coated my
hand and arm with lambing lubricant and gently investi-
gated.

It was clear that the softer life suited Lamb Chop to such
an extent that she had conceived her first pair of twins but
they were hopelessly tangled together and I couldn't reach
to separate them because her muscles were not sufficiently
slackened. Every so often I went out and tried again, but to
no avail. I trudged through the snow to Jim's but he only

confirmed my own opinion that what Lamb Chop needed was a vet – and quickly.

I began the slow trek round all the neighbouring farms. Nobody's telephone worked. The snow-plough driver from Osmotherley must have sliced the cable before the blizzard beat him back and now it would take a JCB to dig a way up to us. The snow had stopped, the wind had died, but the stillness that succeeded it somehow mocked my total powerlessness. One of my oldest friends was distressed and in trouble and not only could I do nothing myself but I could not get help to her from anywhere else.

So here was the classic situation – real soap opera stuff; the road was impassable, the telephone out of action and expert help needed desperately. Between Lamb Chop and our own vet in Northallerton stretched God alone knew how many miles of spectacularly drifting snow. I went to see Jim's other son, Sid, who drives our local snow-plough and he confessed a little shamefacedly that he had hired out his own JCB to a farmer in Hawnby, four miles in the other direction. Now that it had stopped snowing he was going to try to plough his way through to Hawnby and bring the digger back. 'Can I go with you?' I asked. There was a chance after all that there might be a working telephone in Hawnby.

Sid ploughed through to Hawnby with me standing in the transport box behind, throwing shovelsful of salt and grit in our wake. It was early evening before I stood in the tiny village telephone box telling my troubles to a lady vet in Helmsley – a perfect stranger – who said she would try to get through as far as Hawnby if we would wait for her there and conduct her back over the moor road to my home. When she arrived I got in her Landrover and we followed the JCB back through the freezing dark. We could only get as far as Sid's house, but there she cheerfully climbed into waterproofs and wellies and followed me the half mile to where Lamb Chop waited, exhausted and miserable.

It was a hard and lengthy business, a relaxing injection followed by an hour of careful manipulation of the tangled twins like guddling for trout in a hot dark pond and adding our own despair to that of the poor sheep, who suddenly seemed very old and very small in the light of the oil lamp hanging from the rafters.

But by the time I walked back with the vet to where she had left the Landrover there lay beside the tired sheep two big lambs, only just breathing but coming round gradually in the pool of warm light under the infra-red lamp that had sprung wonderfully into life as the power was restored, and in my pocket I could feel the little twist of paper that George had given me earlier in the day when I was searching for help – half a dozen of his backache pills; the only muscle relaxant he had to offer! I don't know whether I would ever have tried them but the thought was there and it warmed me on the way back home after seeing the vet safe, to know that I was not the only person in the world daft enough to care about Lamb Chop, the oldest moor ewe in Upper Ryedale.

I went back into the barn. There was Lamb Chop and her two babies – a son and a daughter, and all three of them seemed barely alive. Within an hour or two the tup lamb folded up like a little flower and died without a fight. I could not save him.

Lamb Chop was disinclined to stand, firmly refusing both food and drink and the gimmer lamb, a real beauty, had about as much get-up-and-go as Elizabeth Barratt in

Wimpole Street. I called her Madeleine, after the vet who had saved her life, and I devoted most of my efforts for some time after that to ensuring her survival, which at times seemed doubtful.

Lamb Chop hadn't a drop of milk. The supply had been ready on tap when the enterprise began but after her ordeal she could not be persuaded to yield even a trickle. A mixture of psychological factors and hormone disturbance no doubt, but understanding the mother didn't help the child and there was a nagging little thought at the back of my mind that this was somehow typical of Lamb Chop with her sky-high buggeration factor. Old Snuff, I told myself, would never do such a thing; her teats would drip at the very sound of a hungry lamb. And it was to her that I turned for help.

Snuff herself had lambed the day before. I found her in the old cowbyre fast asleep. Her huge lop-eared terry-towelling daughter lay smug and full beside her and she herself gave no more than a sigh of resignation as I swung her up on to her haunches, bent over and milked out just enough for Lamb Chop's little one into a Mickey Mouse eggcup.

I didn't go to bed that night. I dozed in the chair, getting up at intervals to steal a drop of milk for Madeleine. Soon both Snuff and her child got wise to these visits and as soon as she heard the door open the lamb would fly in and suck and suck and twirl her catkin tail, desperate to guzzle as much as possible before I took the rest.

As soon as the roads were clear I got an injection for Lamb Chop that brought back her milk supply. But as soon as her lamb began to suck, down she went with acute lambing-sickness and I had to inject her with calcium to save her life. The poor old sheep must have been like a pincushion by now.

She rallied spectacularly but then it was the lamb's turn. She failed and became sickly. Her little legs folded like spaghetti on a fork and she whimpered and snivelled in a corner while Lamb Chop, who had till then been utterly indifferent to her, suddenly realized that this was, after all, the lamb that Nature had prepared her for and she bleated and fretted and would not leave the little one alone.

Pain, distress, hot swollen joints – a sort of septic arthritis known to shepherds as 'joint ill'. Another, different, course of injections.

But at the end of the following week, when the snow had melted and I could get about again on my moped, I came back from a trip to the village to find Lamb Chop waiting for me in her usual place by the gate, just outside the hen-hut where I kept the moor sheeps' food, as though the nightmare had never happened. It was just like old times, except that she was no longer alone. Madeleine sat beside her, cuddled up to her shoulder, rehearsing her mother's deliberately winsome expression. A glance passed between them.

I knew then the answer to the question someone had asked me not long before. 'Old Snuff's made you quite a bit of money over the years, but I bet Lamb Chop's spent most of it. You should ask yourself, Missus, is she worth it?'

I looked at the self-satisfied pair and said 'Yes.'

'Yes what?' Lamb Chop seemed to be asking, but I didn't tell her.

We lost Lamb Chop the following February. Something caused her unborn lamb to die and the shock was too much for her poor old system. Despite treatment, she died quietly, with her head on my knee, at about eleven o'clock on a

Tuesday morning.

And nothing happened. No crash of thunder, no sudden eclipse. No indication at all that Nature had taken the slightest notice of an event of such monumental gravity. It went on snowing fitfully as the little sheep who had shared fifteen years of our lives just left quietly, like an old lady stepping off a bus, leaving us to go on without her.

I didn't cry. I settled her gently into an attitude of sleep and left her; she didn't need me any more.

While she lived on the moor she had organized her own life while letting me believe I was running it for her, but for the last few years I had turned the tables, successfully and surreptitiously easing her old age. I had loved her dearly; now she was gone. But still I didn't cry. I went for a walk with Turpin up on to the moor and we wandered until we found our young sheep grazing in the snow-flurries around the green mossy well that had once supplied water for the old village school. One of them was Madeleine and I watched her for a long time, remembering, without tears.

On the way back I looked into the hen-hut to see whether there were any letters. One, forwarded from the Evening Post. There was something lumpy inside which turned out to be a magnet.

The year before, the very week before Lamb Chop's narrow escape – I had written in my column about cherished memories of childhood toys and how I had searched in vain for a magnet like the one I had treasured as a child. And now, a whole year later, a reader had remembered. Someone had found exactly the same red, chunky magnet which clunk-clicked on to the fat little ingot that stopped its magic from escaping into the corners of my pocket, and had sent it to me.

On that Tuesday night, over and above the chilly snow-scape, there came a sunset that was just too cruelly perfect for such a day. I had gone to put a gate on the little shelter where Lamb Chop still lay as I had left her, so that nothing could defile the corpse before I could dig a proper grave for her. As I stood and stared, the whole long ridge of the Hambleton Hills, a dim row of sleeping white elephants, was outlined with the special scarlets of Superstar roses and Surefire geraniums, as though beyond their protective barrier the rest of the world were on fire. Lamb Chop was dead. I had accepted that. Now suddenly I realized that she was no longer alive, and somehow that is not quite the same thing.

And then I cried, and my fingers closed round the little red magnet in my pocket and I clutched it in my fist till my palm ached almost as much as my heart.

When I first started keeping sheep I bought a little blue notebook in which I wrote the names and numbers of my first few precious lambs. As the years went by I added list after list – who begat whom, when each sheep was sheared, who was sold and for how much, and which sheep-dip I used and when. It is a complete record of the triumphs and disasters of fifteen generations of woollen friends, and although it is of no material value except to me and possibly the Ministry of Agriculture, I should hate to lose it. On the very first page is recorded the arrival of a 'black Suffolk-cross, bought of Mr W. Raw for one pound'. And the name – Snuff.

After more early setbacks than the sickliest child in Victorian melodrama she became part of the farm as it grew from a daydream to a way of life and gradually took her place at the very heart of it. She had figured in all my books, appeared on television and was mentioned so many times in my columns that most of Leeds looked upon her as partly theirs. And now I have come to write the last chapter of her story.

One Wednesday afternoon, after a feast of Granny Smiths and digestive biscuits, good old Snuff fell quietly and permanently asleep with her head in my lap and my face buried in the great ruff of springy wool round her neck into which I have poured so many of my tears and troubles over the years. Under the plum trees in the orchard in the place she loved to lie, I said goodbye at last to my old friend.

But I am not asking you to feel sorry for me so much as to forgive me, because she belonged to my readers too, and when she died it was by my hand.

She seemed to have been a very old sheep for a very long time. During the previous summer she had begun to limp, slightly at first and then worse until she seemed to walk with difficulty and solemn determination, dragging her stiff hind legs. I used anti-arthritic drugs for a while with some success, and even explored the possibility of joint replacement surgery, but the vet said that the spinal deterioration was irreversible. She was in no pain but walking any distance became a Herculean effort.

During the winter this was no problem; she was not in lamb and there was no need for any more exercise than she could manage. I carried her food to her and she lacked for nothing. With a little help she would totter out when the weather was reasonable to share the company of Lamb Chop who never strayed far from the house for reasons of greed. When Lamb Chop died Snuff really seemed to miss her, though perhaps that was my imagination. It is always a little too easy to credit animals with feelings that are our own.

I had often said that I would put the old sheep down rather than 'send her in' when she ceased to enjoy being alive, somehow knowing that I would know, that she would tell me when the time was right. Not right for me, but right for her.

Spring came suddenly in a flurry of hot and hazy days. The lambing was nearly over but this year there was no lamb for Snuff to treasure. Now and again she would lift her head in response to a faraway cry. The grass began to grow and all around the tired and winter-weary creatures began to wander in search of the first precious green shoots. Snuff picked about alone among the plum trees, unable to drag her tired old body in pursuit of one more spring.

And I knew that it was time. My greatest fear for my own old age is the time when I can hear the familiar calls and have no longer the power to heed them. The time when spring makes me sad.

I asked the vet for an injection that would ensure a peaceful passing for a good old friend and late on that Wednesday afternoon, when all the neighbours were at market and we had the dale to ourselves, I set her spirit free.

The very last page in the little blue book is a triumphant list of the new lambs born that spring, but on the inside of the back cover it says simply: 'Snuff. RIP'.

8

Long Hilltop Striding

To walk on hills is to employ legs
To march away and lose the day.
Confess, have you known shepherds?
And are they not a witless race,
Prone to quaint visions?
Not thus from solitude
(Solitude sobers only)
But from long hilltop striding.

From *To Walk on Hills* by Robert Graves

I never quite got over the feeling that the time I spent walking on the moors was somehow stolen, but I could not decide from whom, so was never able to justify the feeling – or the theft.

Of all the lovely things that bound me to the lifestyle I had dreamed and created, the freedom of the high places was perhaps the most wonderful. The dilapidated farm, the small, ill-shaped fields I had created from garden plots and roadside verges, these were beloved responsibilities; but the great moor with its rough-and-ready roads that led away from them like primrose paths from the ways of righteousness was both temptation and reward.

At first when the moor called I seldom answered because I had to account for the time I had spent in the absence of the head of the household. To say that I 'went for a walk' was to bring down a cascade of recrimination. A stiff finger would alternately point to what had been left undone and poke hard into the places to right and left of my chin that were not quite shoulder and not quite breast.

Then, gradually, as the marriage cooled and thinned, there was more and more time that I could ease away from duty and with Andy at school I loaded Robert and Nan into their old high pram and pushed them for miles, looking and learning. And when the marriage ended and my new role as a single parent began, I was eventually able to shift the focus so that one by one the joys became duties in themselves. Simple. Subtle.

It took me a long time to really understand that I was now in the driving seat, in sole charge of the family that was trundling down a fairly predictable sort of road when the driver baled out. For a while it was as though I were still in the passenger seat, leaning across and steering awkwardly but eventually I changed my metaphorical vehicle so that I was no longer trying to span two seats; I was alone in front, in the middle, in charge and in control. I had mentally changed the car for a tractor and I realized that I could take it wherever I liked; that provided I ensured the safety of my three precious passengers, off-road was OK. I was on a high; I felt like Toad – '*Poop-poop!*'

It was in that spirit that the farm was begun. Not in defiance or self-sufficiency, just a conviction that the good life and the happy life were one and the same thing and that no lasting benefit was ever derived from angry competition, no worthwhile lesson ever learned from arbitrary comparison. I had smelt pure joy in this place, in this way of life and I simply longed to try it on, like new shoes.

One of the more emetic phrases used by dabblers in the New Age culture is 'Strangers are only friends we haven't met yet.' In the Dale there was a more honest maxim, though it was lived-by rather than stated: 'Friends of less than twenty years are only strangers we've decided to give a chance to.' We lived there, but that didn't mean we belonged. Because the moor was part of a National Park, I could walk on its paths whenever I liked, but in order to share in it I needed a stake in it; I needed sheep on it.

To turn sheep out on to the moor – the 'common' as it was known – you had to be the holder of a *bona fide* 'stray'. That meant a right to graze an agreed number of sheep on the unfenced moorland and a duty to share in all the communal responsibility in return. The moor strays went with the farms, and since I only lived in the abandoned house while Jim still farmed most of the land that had once belonged to it I would have to have a special, new stray created for me. This would give me a place on the team but first I had to earn it. The opposition was fierce; strays were part of the land and to share was to give away.

Other books tell of how I watched, listened and learned and how I turned my few waifs and foundlings into a flock; of how the landlord granted me a special right to grazing on the common for a small fee per head, so that he did not threaten the rights of the other tenants and I became a hill farmer at last. Technically I now had a right to share the moor but to the end I preferred to regard it as a privilege, afraid of losing the sweet taste of wickedness that accompanied the first step beyond the intake wall.

Part of that wickedness was the sharing of the company of the other farmers. Wives who were told that their place was at home fettling the dinner were angry that I was tolerated in places where they were unwelcome. The fact that they held other exclusive privileges with regard to these same farmers seemed to be of no account; in fact this was one of many aspects of my place in the community that was paradoxically considered to be both sexually inappropriate and sexual misappropriation. Their minds were never set at rest by the undercurrent of male gossip to the effect that I was probably not normal as far as my gender was concerned.

But normal is a word without much meaning in the area of human sexuality where there are no rules, only imperatives. Perhaps the women who feared my carefully cultivated sexlessness were aware of something that I never spoke of; the fact that when I was dressed as a man, working among men, holding my own on their terms, I felt more wholly female than in any other circumstances. The smell of the shearing-shed – grease, sweat and Stockholm tar – still hurts me now in places other than my heart and my head.

Much of the time I spent on the moor was shared with my dog, my sheep and my words. Up there I had the freedom to try out my thoughts aloud, to go back and change and repeat them until they made sense. I think that is where I began to make poetry, although I saw it then only as a sort of spoken shorthand or as the place my thoughts had got to when they grew tired and called fainites.

The hill farmer's calendar sets aside plenty of time for solitary walking. Each spring, when the ewes come in off the moor for lambing, their daughters from the previous year – the gimmer hoggs – go out in their place and for the next month they have the moor to themselves. During this time they have to be hefted – trained by the shepherd to take a certain route each day, to get to know the portion of the moor that their mothers and grandmothers have claimed. To come back at night to the gate they were driven out of in the morning, where they will be fed and fêted so that gradually they associate the gate with safety and largesse. They learn, too, the call of their own shepherd and these are the rules that will save their lives in a long hard winter or a sudden storm. Little pigeons are hatched with their homing instincts; sheep have to be taught theirs.

It begins with an hour after dinner. The shepherd will attend to his lambing flock and then, after he has eaten, he'll go up into the intakes – the fields below the moor wall – where he has installed the gimmers, with a hay-rack and troughs. He will open the gate and let them out on to the heather. Each day he will drive them a little further, watch over them a little longer before bringing them home.

The next step will be to let them out before dinner and leave them unattended up there before going up later to find them, gather them and bring them back for the night. I always found this stage terrifying. It was always so hard to let them go, even for a little while. Often I would just take sandwiches and lie down in the heather, sometimes drifting off to sleep if it was warm enough and waking to a warm wipe from Turpin's tongue. Running to find where the hoggs had strayed to, spotting them, counting them, calling them and the relief and the triumph when they heard and turned and came home are sensations I still hold in my heart. The Bible suggests that this is the way Our Lord felt about sinners and I sometimes wonder how anyone who has not had the care of their own sheep can ever understand the significance of it.

Gently, little by little, the grazing range of the young sheep is extended as the days grow to accommodate it. And it is during this vital time in the lives of the mountain breeds that some clown in Westminster decrees we shall change our clocks. I never found a way of explaining to the hoggs that it was now four o'clock even though their brains and bellies told them that it was three, so I gave in, acknowledged that they had the right of it, and let them take a bite out of my evening because I took such pleasure in their daily return and in the sight of them bobbing in single file along their own track in their own time that I could not bear to spoil it. We had struck a bargain, my sheep and I, a bargain too sweet to forfeit to some arbitrary human idiosyncrasy.

So you will understand that over several generations the flock of any particular farmer will have its own routes and paths, its own places to shelter and its own timetable, so that the bulk of the flock can usually be found in an emergency even though the moor has thousands of unfenced acres wherein they might, in theory, be. Of course, some wander. Some stray. Some are chased or gathered in accidentally by other farmers whose dogs run wide. But the majority of them will be found in the area on which they have been hefted.

My own sheep ran on Iron Howe and the soft slopes of Arnsgill Rigg, where a magical spring rises among the stones of a ruined settlement built by the Brigantes when the whole of North Yorkshire was forest and wolves still prowled in it – or so the story goes.

And up on the moor went many stories, most of which had gained much in the telling. One of the older farmers had it that the deep ditches just above the intakes were the work of Oliver Cromwell's army, but I was not sufficiently convinced to drop this into the conversation with the fertilizer magnate. I felt they probably had more to do with the firebreaks that were created in the early fifties when one of Yorkshire's worst peat fires seared acres of moorland down to bare rock and the farmers had their strays reduced until the heather recovered.

I believe it was the same chap who told me that the tall stone on Cow Rigg engraved with a letter T was the place where a long-ago lover by the name of Tyreman trysted with his girl and carved his initial while he waited. Observation told me that it was one of a line of such stones, all similarly engraved, and books told me that they marked the line below which turf could be dug.

The skyline was dominated by the giant Bilsdale transmitter, so tall that it had to be lit at night to avoid damaging aircraft. Jim told my children that it was he who drove there every day at dusk in his Landrover and shinnied up it to light the lamps and for a little while they believed him.

Gathering was especially exciting. Because I had sheep of my own on the moor, I went with the other farmers to gather down the rigg when it was time to bring them in for dipping, tupping and lambing, but nearly always I would go up by myself beforehand and put my own sheep safe inside, trading on the old promises between us. Sometimes one or two would be missing and I would search eagerly

for them among the great draft of woollen souls that fun-
nelled down in front of the line of men and dogs and me.

We would start early, meeting at the moor gate. I would
arrive at the rendezvous ridiculously early, afraid of being
left behind, knowing that if I were not there nobody would
wait.

The other farmers would turn up in their own vehicles
but only one would be taken higher up and parked by the
ruckle, the untidy pile of stones at the top of Cow Rigg.
Usually it was either Jim's Landrover or George's. I was
always in the back with the dogs. Most of the summer gathering took place on wet days, because dry ones were dedi-
cated to the getting of hay, especially when they were few
and far between, as was often the case. The wet dogs would
smell like imperfect wine and the gusts of their unsavoury
breath would alternate with the incoming draughts of peat
and heather and the background fug of old, warm, wet
waterproofs.

From the ruckle we all walked the outer perimeter of the
moor. One by one the farmers would stop and take their
positions, each at a high point where he could see the next
man. We'd leave George at Joseph Wade's hut, then Jim and
I would walk along the stiff clay track to Bilsdale bank top
and I would wait at the stone ruckle there while Jim went
down to the wall below.

As soon as I saw the sheep begin to run up from the gully
below the wall that formed the moor's western boundary I
would begin to walk down driving all the sheep in front of
me. I would give a wave to George and he, too, would set off
downwards, casting his two dogs to left and right to keep
the sheep running, and the other farmers bringing in the
sheep from the eastern side would converge to meet them.

We, I once decided, became the walking hypotenuse of a triangle whose right angle was formed by the length of that western wall and the moor's lower boundary. As we came down the moor driving the sheep before us their numbers seemed to grow as the area of the triangle diminished and those three theoretical squares shrank in proportion to our downward progress. It is in ways like this that walking up high in fresh air turns the brain.

The sounds, too, come together as the sheep move down from the high places. The distant whistles, far-off and spaced-out are superseded by gruff verbal commands; *Come by! Lie down!* and, when now and then a crafty ewe slips through the cordon and heads back whence she came, *Get back, ye bugger!* The occasional calls of one ewe to her cronies become the constant, panicking cries of mothers and young who have lost each other in the great boiling mêlée as the gather reaches its destination, and when one man has fought a way through the desperate throng to open the gates into the intake, they spill in like porridge boiling over the lip of a saucepan and the bleating dies slowly down as the lost ones find each other and settle to graze and suck.

But the best times of all were spent walking for the walking's sake, often side by side with Jim, our dogs fossicking in the heather as we went. Sometimes we'd walk for miles in silence, sometimes we'd talk so hard putting the world to rights that we'd arrive in some high, familiar place with no recollection of the getting there.

As soon as Turpin could toddle, he came up on the common and would follow till his legs got tired, whereupon I would pick him up and carry him, first in my pocket and later in my arms until the day came when he could take the long, brittle heather in his four-legged stride. Once, when he was small, I suddenly noticed that he was not at my heels and called to Jim to stop. We could see no sign of him. Then on the thin wind came a heartbroken howling and we ran back to find him in the bottom of a deep ditch that we had stepped over without thinking. I shuddered to think what would have happened had we wandered out of earshot before I noticed he was missing and his preciousness made me suddenly vulnerable. I had for a moment taken the moor for granted and been taught a lesson. I held my beloved pup close, promising that there would not be a next time.

Jim always maintained, referring to the bloody-mindedness of the livestock, that people who kept moor ewes never got to heaven. But working up there, sorting sheep in a shimmering heat haze or striding out along the rigg with the wind's help, it occurred to me that for such a man there was no better place than this anyway.

Right at the top of the moor is a place where it drops away down into Bilsdale and the great escarpment is known locally as The Clough. Now and again when the weather was especially fine we would wander up there, just to see if any of our sheep had got that far. The high point above The Clough was known as Jackdaw Rocks and one day we sat there, talking over matters of consequence when Jim asked me how it felt to be famous. He was referring to my recent television appearance and to the short, doomed infatuation with the producer which I had confided. I threw a stone down into The Clough and watched it clatter out of sight. I did not want to talk about it. 'Cheer up,' he said. 'When you get really well known there'll be any amount of shiny-shoe boys queuing up to take you out and give you a good time.' And he rose to go.

We walked in silence for a while, he striding and I scuttling behind, trying at the same time to comprehend and to ignore. Suddenly I felt a sickening collapse beneath my foot and knew without looking what I had trodden on. I knelt beside the ruined clutch of woodcock eggs. 'Now you've done it,' said Jim. It was one of his favourite phrases.

'Yes,' I said, trying not to cry. 'Will she lay another clutch?' 'No,' he said, 'it's too late for that.' And neither of us spoke again until we were in sight of the moor gate.

Turpin's twin sons grew up fit and strong. I had by then begun to spend more time away from the farm during the day and decided to keep one so that Turpin would have something else to look after when I wasn't there. Donovan, black and white and bouncy was the more outgoing of the two. He was a born winner, always at the best teat. When he had drained it he would take Dylan's, pushing him further back. When they were weaned he would bolt down his own food and then steal Dylan's. Dylan never objected. If a visitor came Donovan would bound up and perform while Dylan would sit still, wagging his tail, waiting. When the time came to send one of them away, there was no contest. Donovan could take care of himself, I reasoned – and anyway, dear, easy-going Dylan was simply too special to part with.

He was an odd little thing, with his father's collie body on his mother's Queen Anne legs. He had great ginger ears like chrysanthemums and was a collector of small things, especially socks, which he hid in his special hole under the old stone trough in the yard. Once he carried a kitten, quite safely, and tucked it carefully away with his other treasures.

He soon became a cheerful, biddable adolescent and then he often went walking on the high moor with his father and me. One day, just before I had finally admitted to myself that I had decided to run away, I was setting off up to the moor gate when Mart, his Lordship's gamekeeper, called gracelessly 'Oi!'

When I went back to see what he wanted, smiling in anticipation of his usual pleasant conversation, he looked sourly at me, then at Dylan, and said 'You can't take that thing on t'moor.' I asked why ever not. He raised his voice; 'Because it's not a sheep dog. It's got no right up there. Go on, take it back to t'house.' The expression on his face was one of unpleasant authority. Shaken, I turned and went home.

To this day I have never understood what prompted that outburst. Dylan had never been in mischief. Besides, any visitor's dog, under control, is allowed within the National Park. I often wish I had stood my ground that day, and found out what made Mart behave like that, instead of turning round and leaving him there among his entourage of fat little terriers.

9

The Beginning of the End

A Moment's Halt – a momentary taste
Of Being from the Well amid the Waste—
And lo! — the phantom Caravan has reach'd
The Nothing it set out from — Oh, make haste!

The Rubáiyát of Omar Khayyám
Translated by Edward Fitzgerald

I can remember the day that the end began. It was early
December, 1986. I had been out on my little motorbike to
visit Nan in her digs in Northallerton and when I came back
to the farm, engine off, legs trailing decadently, singing,
coasting down the hill, everything had changed.

A large white caravan was parked at the bottom of Jim's
field, just outside my gate. It was parked so near my fence
that I could touch them both at once and its wide picture-
window overlooked my yard. What on earth could have
happened? Nobody I knew would park a caravan without
asking and for somebody I didn't know to put one so close
to the habitation of someone who had neither been warned
nor consulted seemed inconsiderate and rude.

I went straight along to Jim's farm, truculent and muttering, rehearsing my wholly justifiable complaint. I would 'tell on them', whoever they were, and Jim would make them move. Jim had a relaxed attitude to campers and would always give permission to anyone who came and asked, but he would never have told anyone to camp right outside my home. Not Jim.

Jim explained, not quite meeting my eye. The new estate manager, Stuart Sutherland, of whom more anon, had started a campaign to tidy up the estate and was using supervised gangs of community service 'volunteers' on a programme of dry-stone walling along the footpaths and bridleways to which the public had access. They had been working for weeks around the picnic area on the road past Jim's place and were now starting on the green lane that linked the row of farms along the hillside. My farm was central and they would be using the caravan as a base.

I heard myself howling 'But they *can't*'. I was in tears and Jim was embarrassed. 'Sutherland asked if they could put it there and I can't see how it makes any difference to you.' He stumped off to get on with something he hadn't been doing when I arrived and I felt myself dismissed.

My heart was beating too fast and my stomach felt as if it had come untethered. Did he really not understand how uninvited presence, inescapable proximity would make me feel? I turned to go, still sobbing.

Jim called after me 'Anyway, it's not worth making such a bloody fuss; that's my best meadow and they'll have to be off by the time I need to be on with the grass harrows.' I felt worse. Jim wouldn't be harrowing the grass till after he'd taken the cattle off and that wouldn't be till May. I determined to ask Mr Sutherland to re-locate the caravan.

In the event, it stayed where it was for the proverbial year-and-a-day.

Stuart Sutherland was one of the more radical innovations to hit the dale upon the retirement of his predecessor and he hit it with the deep, dull impact of a brick in mud. Whatever college of estate management he attended had polished him smooth and hard and he clearly did not see the likes of me as an asset worth preserving. He stood huge between the tenants and the landlord cutting off an avenue of appeal we had come to take for granted. He was a handsome and intelligent young man, but his face was as new to me as was mine to him. We both fell short when measured against each other's expectations. Within a very short while I feared and disliked him; it took a long time to accept that he viewed me with irritation and distaste.

I asked if the caravan might be moved and he pointed out that it was not on my property. I tried to explain what it would mean to me to be under constant observation, overlooked, overheard. He appeared not to understand.

And on the Monday after the caravan arrived, the nightmare began. I had been up early to feed the sheep and had settled at my typewriter to put together my weekly letter to Leeds. There was a slight disturbance among the poultry. Turpin ran to the door and we went outside together. Gathered around the caravan twenty yards from my door were six or seven men and at the sound of the door opening they turned as one. And looked at me.

Turpin began barking like a thing possessed and I called him back into the house and shut the door fast. I leaned against it, shaking, plucking up the courage to go out and ask the men to move the caravan. I knew they would not go away altogether, but I could show them a place only a dozen yards to the right where we would not be visible to each other. Surely I could make them understand that for a singular and solitary person to go to bed in splendid isolation and wake up in the middle of a small housing estate was like being sent to hell. With Turpin beside me, I went out to meet my tormentors.

Under the eyes of the uninvited assembly I walked the distance between us. I said my piece; the foreman said my proposed site wasn't flat enough and changed the subject. 'I hope that dog's safe.'

'So do I,' I said, knowing that if anyone dared lift a finger to my beloved Turpin I'd spill their blood. 'We'll be coming and going through your yard,' he said, 'so you'd better keep it under control.'

'Oh, no,' I said, reasonably. 'The footpath runs down below the house,' but he said that Mr Sutherland had told him he was to use my yard as a thoroughfare, so as to avoid the mud. 'But we *live* here,' I shouted, as though that would explain everything. 'What's the matter?' he said, and I realized that I was crying again.

What was the matter with me? The row of eyes above the condescending grins suggested that it was something pretty fundamental. They clearly thought I was not quite right in the head. I fumbled for words that they might understand, for ways to tell them that the quality of my life would be irretrievably diminished if they were parked in the middle of it. But I failed and they stayed.

Perhaps they were right; perhaps I was more than a little mad. They saw me as over-reacting to an inconvenience but I felt bereaved and betrayed. So many of the simple things that I had taken for granted for so long became lost and lamented luxuries. I used to play in the pond like a toddler, barefoot and safe. I used to walk for hours up and down the yard, talking and singing where nobody could hear me.

But from that day on it was all spoilt. Each time I opened the door to go out I peeped first to see if the coast was clear, holding the dog back with my knee so that he wouldn't slip out and alert the enemy. Whenever I could I sneaked along the front of the house and over the far wall, so as not to have to pass them. Sometimes, though, I could not avoid passing the caravan when it was occupied, and I never got used to the sickening surge of humiliation each time the sickle profiles swivelled into a row of pink moons, each with two inquisitive eyes which followed me as I went to attend to the pigs or the poultry.

When I was a child, in a London garden, I used to live out a million fantasies down among the raspberry canes, but I was always aware of being benignly observed, now and again hearing my own play quoted, conscious of, and resenting, the well-meaning smiles – 'she'll play for hours like this, you know . . .' Once, when I tried to explain this to my mother, she said; 'If you feel like that you'd better go off and live in the middle of nowhere.' And I did. And look what happened.

I felt suspended, incapable and unsure. I disliked staying at home because it wasn't home any more and I was reluctant to go away for fear my beloved creatures came to harm. I did not think my visitors would be deliberately cruel but I knew they were capable of churlishness and stupidity. One day in a clumsy attempt at reconciliation the foreman said that he understood why I was upset – 'it's having all these handsome young men around when you're not used to it' – and I felt my hands balling into fists in my pockets.

And now nothing I treasured was truly mine any more.

The lads, amiable enough but thick and uncouth, commented and pointed, honking and hooting at my poultry, imitating my old lame sheep and snoring at my pigs like the worst kind of children in the saddest kind of zoo as they trailed back and forth to the site of their activities, their daily stint of thoughtless *blitzkrieg* and arbitrary reconstruction.

And on one awful evening I went outside to find the foreman giving a strange young lady, presumably a probation officer, a guided tour of my outbuildings. I listened to him, appalled . . . 'And this is Bob the Rabbit. He's a real character is Bob when you get to know him. Here, you can stroke him if you like . . .' and I ran back into the house and flung myself on to the sofa, howling hopelessly.

It wasn't *fair* – even in stately homes the punters paid their half-crowns. And even now I find it difficult to express how very much it mattered that the rabbit's name was Tom.

I realize what it was now, that thing that began to eat into everything that I had worked so hard to create, to become. I was being forced to look at my life in the light of other people's reality and I was losing my faith in my own. After so much blessed self-containment I had forgotten that the real world is an uncertain place; when these people gatecrashed my private party they invited the world in with them and my own frail certainty wilted in its shadow. What I called idyll they called fantasy; what I called fantasy they called delusion and although these distinctions were perceived rather than articulated, I felt myself slide from complacency to confusion. Who in hell was I?

But life went on in its altered and threatened form. I adapted to the presence of the invaders in the way whole civilizations have done throughout history. My lifeline was the traditional refuge of the oppressed; legend, myth and self-deception. If I carried on writing to Leeds, perpetuating the belief that my Golden Age still persisted I could keep it safe until it truly came again. *Sic in Arcadia ego.*

Fiercely, single-mindedly, I dismantled damaged bits of the old dream to reinforce what was left. I patched and mended it like a broody goose who pulls her nest into shape around her as she sits. And like all peasants subjected to an alien regime, I began to see conspiracies where hindsight and commonsense tell me that there was only thoughtlessness. Like Job, I failed to recognize that I didn't matter to anyone else half as much as I did to myself. And the more paranoia grew, the greater became my vulnerability.

At the back of the house, behind the derelict farm buildings that adjoined it, was a small square piece of land full of nettles and wild flowers. Over the years it had been a great pleasure to me and to many of the world's smaller and less significant creatures, who found there a safe place where they could simply be, unmolested and gently treasured.

When the children were small and the pile of rubble in the collapsed buildings was a hazard to them, I took it piece by piece and built the wall that separated that small piece of land from all the rest. We called it the pound and it was useful for keeping small things safe: orphan lambs, that were being introduced to grass; sick animals undergoing treatment or simply waiting for the vet; hens with their chicks. Its greatest moment was when Joe Garbutt's Charolais bull came across the river to do battle with Jim's old Galloway, Hadrian. I loved dear easy-going Hadrian and this gave me the courage to push and shove the great beige intruder into my all-purpose enclosure which held him until his owner came with a trailer to take him home.

But even I didn't appreciate just how important it was to me until the foreman of the loathly gang came to tell me that he had had permission from Mr Sutherland to take it down to provide stone for the new wall that was slowly creeping along the green lane towards Osmotherley. He had told them that it 'wasn't serving any useful purpose'.

He said the same thing to me when he came to the farm in response to my appeal. I showed him the guinea-fowl nests in the long grass. He said that if I made sure that all the workers knew where they were they would avoid disturbing them. I knew different. To betray their precious enclaves to that gang of louts would ensure their destruction by peeping and gawping, just like my own. I played my trump card. I took him to a collapsed wall at the top of the hill above the new one. Jim had told me that the workers could have that wall instead of mine. They were better stones and a downhill carry to the site. Sutherland said it was too far and the troops moved in.

As to the guinea-fowl, I stood guard and kept stumm. But when they had taken my wall right down to the foundations I told them not to bother about tidying up. I made it quite clear that I intended to rebuild it. If they wouldn't use Jim's stones, I would.

I began carrying the great flat sandstones one after another down to the house. Gradually the wall of the pound began to reappear, and as I worked, raising the sides, filling in the middle with loose rubble and laying the largest stones across from front to back to tie it all in, the gang came and went without comment. The following Wednesday I cadged a lift to market for myself and half a dozen wether lambs. When I returned, every trace of my new wall had gone. I went into the house and cried like a disappointed child until I was too tired to cry any more, so I started to tidy the dairy.

When one has been feeling really miserable for any length of time, there comes about a sort of weary calm that, in time of need, passes for peace. The old dairy was dark and cool and the dank sweat on the flagged floor smelt of earth. I was safe here.

I came upon an old cracked casserole dish full of chipped and broken treasures too dear to throw away. In it I found a small ornament that Robert had bought me several Christmases before. An extraordinary Dutch milkmaid whose blue and white earthenware posed bravely as Delft while her underneath declared that she was made in Taiwan. When she came there were two tiny buckets that hung on wires from the ends of a yoke across her shoulders. These must have fallen off and got lost in the bottom of the dish. I looked at the fat little figure with the grim oriental features under the winged Dutch hat. Her hands clutched at the ends of the yoke and without the buckets it looked as though she was wrestling purposefully with a Bullworker in an effort to improve her bust.

I thought how deceptive appearances can be and the tears began to flow again as I realized that to the people who had become my tormentors I appeared only as an awkward old woman reduced to snivelling paranoia over a pile of stones. And that there was no such thing as safety. Anywhere.

10
Meg

This ae neet, this ae neet
Ivvery neet an' all
Fire and sleet and candleleet
And Christ receive thy soul. . . .

When whinny muir thou'st crossed unvex'd
Ivvery neet an' all
To meggy mire thou comest next
And Christ receive thy soul

If all thy ducks be in a row
Ivvery neet an' all
Across old Meg thou safe mayst go
And Christ receive thy soul

But if thy ducks be strewn about
Ivvery neet an' all
Old Meg will suck thy daylights out
And Christ receive thy soul. . . .

The New Lyke Wake Dirge

On the great moor above the farm, on the high flat place that is not quite Bilsdale nor really Scugdale, lives Meg.

A familiar, jolly sort of name, Meg. Meg Merrilees, a tan-faced gipsywoman with pegs for sale. A collie bitch, all eye and style, or a farmer's widow, who washes on Mondays and bakes on Friday mornings, filling the air with yeast and spice, wiping the flour from her hands on the hem of her crossover pinny as she scurries out to greet visitors.

But the Meg who lives on Bilsdale Bank Top, at the feet of the television relay mast is not at all of such cheery persuasion. Her home is inviting, all set about with cotton grass and little lawns of lime-and-lemon green, so sharp you can taste it. Welcoming, yes. Positively insistent in fact. But dark, cold and not at all jolly. Cross her threshold at your peril; it you come, you stay.

For this Meg is Meggy-mire. Meg o't' Moors. An extremely large and treacherous peat-bog, reputed to contain, among other things, a Landrover, a horse, still harnessed to the cart that was swallowed up with it, and divers shepherds and their dogs. North Yorkshire folklore is full of such tales of grue; so are North Yorkshire folk, but which governs which I don't feel qualified to say.

There are parallels in the wider world of course. The Shivering Sands, Grimpen Mire, The Slough of Despond. Because they are nightmares of respected fiction we simply accept their malevolence. Meg is real and can be tested. Once I did it; I'm not sure how. I was just suddenly aware, not of danger so much as un-safety. I lost my bearings. Even now I cannot remember the threshold, the point where I handed control to Meg. I cannot have been very far in, but I sank to my thighs, and although I got out I had felt the great wet empty heart of her, and was aware for the first time of the hugeness of fear.

But once you have been almost swallowed and survived and the rough grass at the periphery is no longer terra incognita, it no longer gives the same warning shiver. You find yourself straying nearer to the edge without concern, until the ground rocks under your feet again and the old terror grins at you out of the unexpected dark.

In just the same way, I didn't realize what was happening to me as the cheerful chain-gang, innocent as idiots, wrought their arbitrary changes all around.

I had lived my solitary, secret life for so long, happily accepting change as the only constant within it, that I had been taken totally unawares by the overlapping circles of other people's change. I knew that life in the countryside is a gently progressive spiral with the same constants occurring in any set of twelve successive moons yet never covering the same ground twice and that this was good. Changing scenes and characters were all part of the play that I had believed myself to be producing but when someone else stepped into it and took liberties with the script they took my control away and in the lack-lustre days and dark nights that followed the invasion I did consider the possibility that this might be a cause worth dying for.

I have always been fascinated by kingfishers. I love their old name – halcyon. In the old days people believed that kingfishers nested far out at sea, and that the halcyon days – days of calm and peace – were granted to the bird for bringing up her young. I knew better, out of books. They confirmed my affinity with kingfishers, who dash out from time to time, do what they are best at and impress people briefly, from a nest as muddled and unwholesome as mine.

But until these cuckoos invaded that nest, I was blissfully happy with it; it was perfect because it was all exactly how I had contrived it to be. Stuart Sutherland, with his confident assertions to the contrary, had confronted me with my own grubby reality, my apartness from other people's unsuspected standards. I began to believe that I was not so much sinned against as sinning. I became convinced that it had nothing to do with walls at all; that it was I who, in the eyes of the real world, served no useful purpose. I who was an affront to the visitors. I who was betraying the countryside. And that the world was right.

I knew then only that my own halcyon days were gone for ever. I know now that I had curled myself up into a ball and was rolling uncontrollably downhill into a breakdown.

But I'd been here before and survived.

What did I do? What do I ever do? I began to work on the words inside my head, on the descriptions of myself and my ideas. I told myself a new story until I began to believe it.

This was a technique I taught myself as a tot, when I was snatched from my family, thrust into hospital and then sent to a convalescent home miles away as part of the treatment for primary TB which teenage tests proved that I never had in the first place.

I bore the hospital and the home with the sort of fortitude that five-year-olds seem able to call up from the time before their being. When I came back, though, I was six and my own home made different demands on me and the infant school I had loved before the bad times came was now alien and forbidding.

So I didn't go. Oh, my body went there all right, pale and spindly and delivered to the door in a push-chair. My mouth opened every so often like a little bird to take the cod-liver oil, the Radio Malt, the Parrish's Chemical Food and the Brand's Beef Essence that they shovelled down me in the staff room and I responded in class, often to answer questions, once to cry because my peers had moved their mathematics into double figures and left me behind. But out in the asphalt yard I played alone and in silence. I became a pony. The Little Grey Pony, recounting my own adventures in my head as I went along.

It worked, after a fashion. I know now that it was the sum of those hours clattering my lace-up shoes over the rain-slick playground that added up to the self-centredness, the secrecy, the terror of dependence upon others that are all part of my adult self. Then, though, I knew only the sweetness of escape from my classmates who seemed loud and cruel, and the power of reorchestrating my parallel universe so as to exclude them. I learned how to make safety.

And if I had done it before, I could do it again. It was just a matter of remembering how.

11
Changing the Context

Sometimes I'm in the mood, I wanna leave my lonesome home
And sometimes I'm in the mood, I wanna hear my milk cow moan

Bob Dylan

In the year before I ran away there was much talk in the Dale about the fact that I was preparing my sheep for lambing almost a month before any of my neighbours. I heard from my neighbour Sandra that 'they' – which in my long experience meant Sandra herself – were saying that 'she' – which always meant me – was determined to 'be first'.

This was nonsense, of course. Hill sheep lamb when they do because that is the best and safest time for them to do so. For someone who loved their sheep as I did to change the established order of things would need a pretty good reason and I was disappointed that Sandra and her coterie had not given me the benefit of their collective doubt, and that none of them had taken the trouble to ask me face-to-face why I had so ordered things in the autumn that my sheep were lambing early and thereby flying in the face of centuries of local tradition. Had they done so, I would have shown them the university calendar; I had merely timed their hour of greatest need to coincide with my own spring vacation.

For that was how I had decided to parry the blow that had been dealt to me by the arrival of the caravan on my doorstep. The change that came with it was cruel and unwelcome but I was powerless to do anything about it. I had played stone, scissors and paper till I realized that the only thing that would defeat change was more change; the exchange of bad for good. The reasoning was crude and simple. Fate had pissed on my fireworks. The display I had envisaged was no longer possible. I now had to lay them all out on the table, throw away the ones that were ruined and see what I could make of what was left. My heart was hurt, maybe beyond perfect healing, but I still had my head, more or less. I took a step sideways, away from the ghetto-blasting invaders. I applied to and was accepted by York University to read for a degree in English.

I never for a moment considered giving up the farm; I was convinced I could spin both threads in parallel. After all, I was already stepping out and back for TV appearances, talks and lectures, launches and lunches. Even a part-time job. This would be possible. I thought about it until it became desirable, and with the desire came the determination to make it work.

Not that it was easy. That first winter was a cold and difficult one and although the little moped coped wondrously with snow and ice, it didn't afford its rider much protection. One morning I arrived stark-stiff at Northallerton railway station, took off my gloves, locked the machine and fixed my crash helmet on to the special clip in the steering column. I then moved to unpack the plastic raincoat from the shopping basket. This garment, pink and thin, was actually worn by the abandoned motorcycle while I was in York. I used to stick its stubby handlebars into the sleeves, drape the hood over the basket, cover the rest of the bike with the body, do up the poppers under the seat and then make all secure with a bungee cord wound round and round.

On this particular morning, as I steadied the bike with my right hand and asked my left to reach into the basket for the raincoat, it refused to obey. I discovered that I had locked the base of my thumb into the helmet park and I had to fumble for the key to release it. It didn't hurt a bit. I made my habitual dash for the toilet so as to have a wee and a wash and a warm before my train.

The one-and-only toilet at Northallerton railway station is special. It is designed for all contingencies; wheelchair users, the criminally obese, extended families – come one, come all. It is bigger than many a hotel bedroom, with one washhand basin on the right-hand wall and the single porcelain pan set like a throne at the end of a long approach, right in line with the door. I cannot be the only customer to wonder suddenly, in midstream, whether I had slid the bolt on that distant door and to conclude my business with unseemly haste, in case I hadn't.

On those winter mornings the first thing I did was run the hot tap over my hands which were unable to deal with small change and a student railcard until I had restored their circulation and they would awaken under the warm water with the accompanying exquisite agony that reminded me of junior school, where we wound elastic bands around our pinkies to see who could leave them the longest and bore with stoicism the inevitable pain of their ultimate release.

That morning, though, the agony was worse than usual; I watched in amazement as my left thumb awoke to the fact that it had been bitten by the helmet park and started to bleed in a steady gush all over the immaculate appointments. I issued forth eventually, white and shaken, with my left hand transformed into a paw by profligate mummy-windings of toilet paper. I have the scar still.

But I loved that first term. It was like being left alone in a hotel dining-room with a wedding-buffet laid out and all the guests still in the church. Here were tastes of the many things I could feast on later if I chose. Small helpings of this and that: Anglo-Saxon, Middle English, and a headlong rush through a literary tunnel, touching the walls here and there on the way, for luck: the Book of Job, Oedipus at Colonus, Blake, Yeats, Eliot – just a little of each on a biscuit.

I seemed to be managing all right, apart from the hugeness of the journey, and even that had its compensations. I would have a sandwich and a piece of carrot cake on York station and feel simultaneously wicked and blessed. I bought an ancient push-bike and booked a space for it in the long line alongside the Left Luggage and rode it out to Heslington on the days it didn't rain. I bought a college scarf, delighted to discover that it made a glorious woollen breastplate when riding into a cold wind.

I admit to having been afraid of what my neighbours in the Dale would say about my new venture. They had always shown remarkable generosity whenever I tried to acquire a new skill in the fields in which they were already expert, but they could not understand my grief at the coming of the caravan so had no patience with it, and I had a sneaking suspicion that they might see my reaching for knowledge in which they saw no value as a kind of betrayal. Perhaps deep down I saw it so myself. But at first there was no sign of any difference and I told myself not to be so daft. I was doing most of my work at home and only went to York twice a week for tutorials and the odd seminar.

One damp and foggy day during that first term I heard a disembodied voice say 'Mornin'!' as I walked up to the road to fetch the post and I recognized it as that of Mart the gamekeeper. We were not what you'd call close friends but we talked safely over common ground for a while before we parted, I sending my good wishes to his wife and he asking me to keep an eye open for the roadman's old dog who hadn't been home the night before.

I was concerned, though not unduly. Rip was ever a martyr to his worldly appetite and although the days were long gone when he could actually pursue his purpose to a conclusion, his hind legs not being what they were, he still found the subtle call of a bitch in season as loud and clear and undeniable as anything the running tide held for Masefield.

When he came to the Dale as a fat, black pup he drove the roadman's mother, rest her soul, to distraction. He chased her hens, bounced her beloved cat, fetched sticks from the coalhouse and chewed them on the clip-mats and made mess and muddle everywhere. It was in those days that I taught him, almost by accident, his one and only parlour trick. He would jump at me from some point of vantage like a crazed ninja, all eyes and teeth, and I would catch him as deftly as I could manage. He trusted me totally and I never ever dropped him.

The old lady did not live to see him change from a whizzing pup to a large lolloping dog, but even after she was gone and I visited the house less often, I never did so without performing with him the ritual of The Trick. The roadman called him a 'silly aud bugger' but that was only because Rip would snap at him and at anyone else who tried to lift him from the floor; it was always Our Trick, peculiar to the two of us. A pact. A promise. The older he got the more important it seemed to be to him.

I looked for Rip and called his name on my way back home but there was no sign of him. I told myself Rip would come back; Rip always came back.

Next morning there was a knock at the door and Mart stood there. 'Can you give us a hand a minute?' he said. 'It's t'aud dog. In t'gill.' It seems Rip had wandered once too often along the little stream that ran from his house to the river and had sunk deep in the predatory mud of a cattle crossing.

Rip had growled bravely at the gamekeeper and although it would have been perfectly possible to haul the old fellow out without any real danger from the brown and broken teeth, he had decided to fetch me because, like everyone in the Dale, he knew about The Trick. Rip was up to his chest in icy water but he turned his head at the sound of my voice and although he was by then almost blind, he knew me, I was certain.

He came out with a squelch like the first spoonful of a trifle and the mud settled back into the sad little hole with a sickening smell of degeneration. I held him for a moment or two while the worst of the water dripped from him and then laid him on the dry sack that Mart had brought. He offered to take one end like a stretcher but I wrapped Rip up in it and carried him to the keeper's Landrover, laying the frail old bundle carefully between the sacks of pheasant feed. 'I'll split t'reward wi' ye,' said Mart with a wink, manfully ignoring my tears. And he took Rip home.

I curled up on the floor in front of the fire and wept, because I knew what would be done when Rip got home, and that I would not see him again.

I was still wet and muddy so I put my filthy clothes into the laundry basket and went to the airing cupboard for clean ones. The fresh-washed smell reminded of the days when I helped the roadman's mother with her washing while my children played in her yard. Of the pegging-out of hand-hemmed dusters and vast directoire knickers, of home-made tea-cake when the ironing was done and the fat black puppy who ran off with the clothes pegs.

Subtly, as if to avoid having to explain to myself, I began to do things that would darn the gap between the worlds. I chose areas of study where my knowledge of husbandry would add an edge to my contributions; I filled my pockets with conkers in the university grounds and planted them by the boundary fence, telling myself that they would provide the privacy I needed for my old age. For of course I would still be there at Hagg House.

One of the many things I discovered during that first term was that there is much more to Thomas Stearns Eliot than I had allowed myself to suppose and that perhaps the only place where our world views overlapped was in the matter of the naming of cats. I had been given a tiny kitten.

It had a white face upon whose lips whimsical Nature had superimposed a black cupid's bow. It had dull black eyes as if plastic beads had been pressed into its head with a grubby thumb so that they peered, dark-rimmed, like those of a pensive racoon.

I went with a friend to a fund-raising concert at a village school where a local celebrity sang light classics and a teacher played the guitar. After the concert there was a sale in one of the classrooms: second-hand toys, bric-a-brac, home-made cakes and coffee. It was there that I met the little girl.

A very ordinary sort of face she had, with none of the artless charm of the girl who was helping her on the stall. Mouse-brown hair was pulled back from an undistinguished forehead and fixed with a bright plastic crocodile clip which was much in vogue and worn with a sort of open defiance, parodying the things women wore in furtive secrecy in the days of the Marcel wave. She placed herself firmly in the centre of the group of children who were self-consciously 'helping' at the event and I was drawn immediately to her.

She had an opinion on everything. She spoke sharply to one of the sillier boys who was showing off in the way little boys do, noisily and without finesse, using the elastic bands round a boxed jigsaw puzzle as a makeshift crossbow, firing pieces of Lego at the backs of grown-ups. We exchanged glances and started talking. About her family, her teachers, the silly things boys do and the way that one is invariably left, at the end of one of these sales, with a table full of jigsaw puzzles. They never seem to sell. Part of the charm of a jigsaw, you see, is that seductive newness, the cellophane wrapping with its wordless promise that all the pieces will be in the box, that it will not disappoint: something that a second-hand puzzle could never guarantee.

As I talked to her I began to realize why she had attracted me so directly, with her solemn pudding face, her utilitarian hairstyle and her slightly supercilious manner. Something in the way she moved, clumsy and down-to-earth, put me in mind of another little girl with just such a face, just such a personality being relentlessly formed by her dawning awareness of her own lack of grace and a determination to find something, anything, to make up for it. It was like looking down the wrong end of a telescope at my own self, starting out.

She took the jigsaw from the boy and put it crossly back on the table. It was a picture of two racoons peering myopically from a tree. I asked the boy what they were and he didn't know, but the little girl, with an air of worldly wisdom that she had not quite perfected (but oh, how soon it would come) said, 'They're cocoons.'

I felt a fingertip touch of fear for my young friend. Did anyone within earshot know better? To my relief nobody spoke up and neither, of course, did I. Very, very soon the world would begin to challenge her self-assurance, poor little girl. I was damned if I was going to set the ball rolling. For the moment she was safe, her self-esteem held tight in a sort of wistful trust by an odd woman she would probably never meet again. And when I got home I informed the unsolicited kitten that its name was Cocoon.

The day came when my tutorial group were expected to undertake a short residential course of special study and for the first time ever I contemplated leaving the farm in the care of neighbours and distancing myself from it in a way that felt somehow wicked and frightening. All the same I knew that if I did not go I would regret it bitterly and so I set in motion a campaign of elaborate preparation leading up to my departure which made the average Everest expedition look like a day trip to Scarborough. I told myself not to feel ashamed. Jim had offered to do whatever was necessary according to my instructions but the alternating waves of guilt and gratitude were strong enough to produce actual nausea when I thought about what I was doing.

But it was only for a few days and after twenty years of helping out with everything that he and my other neighbours would let me try my hand at, I wasn't really asking much. Or so I tried to convince myself as I sorted out the best of the hay and laid in sacks of sheepfeast and supplies of cat food. I wrote and re-wrote instructions using all my arts of précis and paraphrase, gradually simplifying them until I could hand them over without embarrassment.

The things I actually did in my day to day husbandry looked so bizarre written down as imperatives that I could not bring myself to ask someone else to repeat them. The special touching, the expected words and gestures, were inexplicable to anyone except the creatures of whose lives they had become a part. I found it hard to distinguish between routine task and obsessive behaviour and realized that I had never before made that distinction. I felt the ground shift again and the old fear mouthed more questions at me from the shadows. I ignored them.

I gathered the sheep and brought them down from the moor, fastening them in so that they would be perfectly accessible to their minder. I devised a poultry-proof feeder for the cats in one corner of the barn and a cat-proof feeder for the poultry in another. The housecow was resting between lactations and simply needed seeing every day. The only dependants left to provide for in my absence were the dogs, Turpin and Dylan. They would have to go into kennels and I took some comfort from the thought that they would be together.

On the morning of the day I left I took them both over the moor and down to the village, a long, delightful walk which they loved but which was spoilt for me by the thought that I was somehow betraying them, not having been able to explain to them why I would have to abandon them at the other end. I would say to Turpin what I always said when he had to stay behind – 'Busy. Back soon,' like Christopher Robin to Pooh, but I felt a churning in my stomach at the thought; it would be like using a love-token to betray a friend, something which even history cannot forgive. I felt worse as we got further from home. Perhaps it was the altitude starving my brain of oxygen.

The kennels were even better than I had been led to expect. The proprietors were warm and kind with a manifest love of dogs and a tactful understanding of distraught owners. 'Busy,' I said. 'Back soon.'

While I was away I thought often about the creatures. The sight of sheep safely grazing made me well-wish my own and a contented cow made me run again through the possible mischief into which mine might be getting. But I told myself I had done everything necessary to ensure their welfare. I trusted Jim and was comforted.

It was at the oddest times that I missed the dogs. A shaft of sunlight on the corner of a carpet seemed so to lack a drowsy Dylan that I would look twice to make sure and a puddle on a pathway seemed to want his fat footprints to lead out of it and off to adventure. But the need for Turpin's special companionship would catch me unawares at almost any time; those moments in unaccustomed human dealings where a stifling proximity combined with a dizzying distance to make a pain in my head; the times when all my emotional foxholes seemed as though they had been stopped and there was nowhere to go.

It has always frightened me that when important people are parted from me I cannot see their faces in my head. It was the same with Turpin but while I was away I found I could bring back to me small aspects of him in time of need. Sometimes the sound of his toe-nails on tarmac, sometimes the feel of his weight shifting against my leg in time with a gusty sigh. But strangest of all, I found I could call up in an instant the special smell of his kind and clumsy feet.

12

Going Pear-shaped

But long it could not be. . . .

Hamlet, Prince of Denmark, by William Shakespeare

For a while it worked, though. And in surprising ways. I had been so intent on defending my image as a peasant farmer and observing minutely the effect of my sudden studentship on my rural self-image that I was taken unawares by the other side of the equation. The wholeness and centredness of my life as a practising pig farmer, as a working shepherd, gave shape and substance to my student persona. The discovery delighted me.

I was consulted often during studies of Pre-Raphaelite art and literature as to the accuracy of observation in any work relating to livestock and was able to contribute much of use. I found that as both artist and artisan I was respected and I liked it.

In fact the only thing I undertook during my time at university that was less than successful was a paper on 'Shakespeare the Dramatist' to which I had been looking forward. There was to be no examination for this paper; my performance was to be 'continuously assessed', but I was given no opportunity to perform. I realized as the term went on that the youngsters in whose group I had been placed could not envisage me, the plump middle-aged reality of me, playing make-believe games alongside them. They were happy to discuss their projects in my presence and to notify me of their meetings in the refectory, but they couldn't work me into their fantasy. Several times I was told that the scene they had chosen to present did not have a part for me and I did not argue or plead.

The plays as they saw them had no parts for grandmothers and I was able to remember how, at their age, I would have said the same. I did wonder, though, just what it was in my case that they were continuously assessing and hoped it was my understanding.

The little motorbike struggled under the pressure of commuting, but in summer that wasn't so bad. The only worrying thing was a note of protest that issued occasionally from the leaky exhaust and drew hard stares from passersby. No amount of amateur bodging seemed to help so I had it welded back together by a professional. He shook his head a lot and told me that it wouldn't last for long but I pushed to the back of my mind all those Biblical warnings about new wine and old bottles and my own bitter experience of patching split jeans with new denim.

Sure enough, one day as I thundered through Thimbleby the exhaust dropped off altogether and the sweet, staccato farting that had punctuated my progress was replaced by a sudden agonized note from the engine and the squeal of metal on metal. I felt the rear end of the bike go out of control as the tyre went suddenly flat.

I braked gently to a halt and dismounted safely. I pulled the injured bike off the road, looked at it carefully, then walked into Osmotherley to arrange its rescue. As I walked it crossed my mind that I had been lucky to have suffered this mishap while going slowly along a familiar lane. I could just as easily have been immobilized while crossing the A19 – what if I'd been marooned in the fast lane and one of the regulars had been doing ninety round the blind bend at Jeater – I felt simultaneously sick and fortunate.

The incident served to emphasize once again what a dangerous world is the wider one that I had chosen to take part in and for a day or two I felt subdued and thoughtful: how different from the slow, green peace of my own rural surroundings. I hugged to myself the leisure of a whole day at home with no pressing commitments, a day to slummock around the house and later to take my two delighted dogs for an aimless and extended walk.

Down by the river we went, walking the old route that had become part of my memories of the place, reeking of old hurts and happinesses, watching for the flicking shadows of the trout, noting the places where the water was always cloudy and, as always, wondering why. We surprised a mother duck with her young ones and she led them pell-mell to a place of safety, flying sure and true down the middle of the river, then reappearing, a limping, flapping, clumsy creature, pretending to be injured, playing the easy prey, tempting me and the dogs to follow her away from her precious brood. But I called the dogs close and we sat and waited. After a while she appeared on the opposite bank, creeping through the undergrowth and calling quietly as one by one her babies plopped into the water from their hiding-places and scuttled across to join her. 'Paranoia,' as a friend told me once, 'is a survival trait.'

Only when they were all safe and no more than an invisible column moving secretly in the June jungle did we resume our unhurried walk along the damp banks under the alder trees.

We walked a big circle and were almost home, walking along the lane that was now flanked on both sides by the featureless, institutional walls that the community project workers had built, chiselling the stones into submission. Their false, flat faces looked inwards towards the occasional rambler while the faces that looked back into the fields were rough-and-ready and no obstacle whatever to agile and determined livestock. I should imagine that's how Jim's old Swaledale ewe with her fat twin lambs came to be lurking on the lane. She had resisted all efforts to return her to the moor and went just where she pleased. The dogs trotted ahead and I had no idea the sheep was there until we had effectively cornered her at the end of the lane. 'Sit,' I said. The dogs sat.

The ewe looked at them, weighed up her chances, then made her break for freedom back down the lane towards me. I don't think she even saw me. With her babies galloping behind her she came straight for me, relentless as a woollen train bursting out of a stone tunnel.

I yelled at her, she had plenty of room to pass. I flattened myself against the wall but it did me no good. She cannoned into my right leg just above the knee and I flew over her back to land on the heap of redundant stones that the walling gang had hammered into rubble and left piled at the foot of the wall.

I came to slowly. Dylan was pressing close, looking concerned. Turpin was licking efficiently at anywhere he thought might hurt.

I limped home. My shoulder felt shattered. I was bleeding freely from a cut on my cheek and a green-and-yellow bruise was slowly spreading to encompass my right eye. My head throbbed. It hurt most when I laughed, but I couldn't help myself. Fancy escaping serious injury in a motorcycle accident only to be run over by a sheep.

That night I dreamed of the pig and the passage.

Perhaps the hardest string to let go of was the one that tied me to my place in the fixed feasts of the farming calendar. Already I had changed the time of lambing for my own sheep, so as to fit in with something other than my need to be part of what was going on around me. Gradually other things moved further away from me, things began to happen of which I was no longer a part.

It had hitherto been a matter of huge importance to me to be there when anything was going on. This in itself had become a bone of contention in the early days. Extraordinary games had been played, promises extracted from men by their womenfolk that they would not tell me when they would be clipping or dipping or gathering. But, like a canny gun dog who has learned to read the signs, I always knew anyway and bounded up ready to participate whether summoned or not. I had spent twenty years of my life creating the illusion that I was indispensable and now I needed to ease myself free of it. This proved even more painful than I had feared.

I had won my place in the team by instinctive obedience to all the rules of business, although at that stage I had never seen them written down. I made an art form of over-

achievement. I delivered sooner than expected, I antici-
pated needs, I made no demands. I surprised my diffident
employers time and time again with my stamina and com-
mitment. Eventually they began to take me for granted and
I realized that that was what I had been aiming for all
along.

The local vets eventually expected me to be there for the
annual rituals of testing and castrating cattle, though my
own herd was never more than one at a time, with now and
then a calf at foot. Gradually they acknowledged that I had
learnt what they had shown me, and trusted me with bottles of antibiotics, needles, syringes, pills and pessaries,
confident that I could use them properly.

Once I was at George's, helping with a difficult calving
which in the end defeated all our efforts; the vet came and
pronounced that only a caesarian would save both cow and
calf. He laid out the instruments while George and I
awaited his instructions. He was unwell; his hands were
shaky. He arranged a rope sling to prevent the cow from
lying down, explaining that while she remained standing
there was less chance that her rumen would obstruct access
to her uterus. He gave the end of the rope to George and
told him to hang on to it with all his might, then he picked
up a scalpel, handed it to me and said, 'Cut where I tell
you.' The operation was a success and remains one of my
proudest memories.

But now everything had undergone a subtle shift; time
had moved on and privilege had changed into obligation
without my realizing it. In order to continue I needed to
hand some of it back but the guilt that followed my failure
to live up to the expectations I had created almost beggars
belief. I still have a cutting from the *Sun* that someone left

in the hen-hut with my post. It had been torn out and cir-
cled in green felt tip. 'Has country life gone sour for you?'
it asked. 'Has the good life gone bad?' People who felt this
were invited to contact the paper. I held the bit of newsprint
in my hand like a scorpion. The fact that one of my neighbours felt that I felt this was in itself horrible, the fact that
anyone thought I would consider selling my story to the
Sun was distressing. But the uncomfortable suspicion that
the hand that put it there was the big, slow, safe hand of my
beloved Jim – that was the worst of all. *Et tu, Brute?*

I felt guilty, too, for Leeds – or more precisely the readers
of the *Yorkshire Evening Post* – were the friends with whom
I corresponded week after week; the people to whom I tried
always to tell the truth. Since I found it hard to confess to
myself the changes that were taking place in my life and my
attitude to it, I found it hard to write about them.

Oh, I confided everything that was beyond my control. I
told them about the voyeurs and their relentless, clinical
wall and about the children leaving home and the little
spate of deaths among the most precious old retainers. I
wrote about my occasional achievements. But I was less
than honest about the changes that I myself was bringing
about in response to all this. Because I didn't want them to
know.

So many people wrote to me telling me that I was living
out a personal pipe-dream on their behalf. How could I
betray them? I tried to work up a flicker of resentment, but
failed. The most terrible responsibility in the world is someone else's dream.

That last spring was a long time in coming. A fine day for
the dipping of the sheep was hard to find and the decision

to go ahead was taken one grey morning in March. Jim no longer used the old dipping pens near to my house, having built new ones in the fields behind his own. George and I both took our sheep along there early, giving a day's work in return for the use of Jim's dip. It was not long before the first lambs were due.

The dipping was done by midday. After a meal at Jim's George took his sheep back along the road, and I gave him a half-hour start and then followed with mine. As I persuaded the unmotivated, overweight animals back to their lambing field, I scanned the hedgerows for signs of spring. Apart from a couple of muddy snowdrops beside the cattle grid, one of which fell victim to the questing snout of one of my charges, there was none.

It was a warm, damp sort of day which seemed to be wondering whether to degenerate into wetness and deciding it wasn't worth the effort. Along the road we trudged, with the mothers-to-be lagging and dawdling, insisting on inspecting every crisp-packet and sweet-wrapper. Here and there the remains of snow, grey and gritty, still lay under the walls and as we filed along in the warm still air between the high hedges there was no sound except the clacking of hooves on tarmac and over everything hung the damp-sock smell of freshly-dipped sheep.

Halfway home one of the heaviest of them lay down with a deep sigh and insisted that she wasn't going another step. I took handfuls of wool at her neck and loin and lifted her, trying to set her on her feet but she stretched her neck forward and made her legs go all floppy so that the minute I let go she slummocked down again on the road, 'sulking' as the local shepherds call it. But she was breathing very heavily and her lambing was only days away, so I lifted her off the carriageway and left her to have a breather while the rest of us kept up some sort of forward progress, strung out along the road. Sure enough, the fear that she might be missing something overcame her weariness and she soon caught up with the rearguard.

That was the only trouble with the 'biblical' style of shepherding that I had developed, where the sheep were led rather than driven. Under field conditions it had huge advantages over the conventional dog-and-stick stuff, but on the Queen's highway it had its hazards. Off I would go down the road with the first two or three hot on my heels, but the tail-end of the flock could be as much as two hundred yards behind, digging in the grit heap for bits of salt or passing the time of day with stranger-sheep behind a gate. If I turned back to chivvy them, the front runners would come back with me and what should have been a dignified progress at a steady rural pace became a mad bleating free-for-all, so I usually carried on steadily to wherever I wanted us all to end up and hoped for the best.

The best, which seldom came about, was a clear road with no cars. Most motorists were reasonably considerate and patient but I was none the less in a position to know just how far along a fenced road two or three panic-stricken sheep could run in front of a car. The worst that could happen was a car coming in the opposite direction driven by the sort of louts who found it fun to chase sheep. After they had passed me and the few who were near enough to me to feel safe, they would send all the rest of them back along the narrow lane in front of them. I have seen many a car-load of these thugs wind down their windows, lean out and beat on the sides of their speeding vehicle, going 'Wooooo-wooooo-wooooo' at the tops of their fag-battered lungs the better to scare the sheep and make them run, eyes popping, tongues hanging, breath rasping until they found a gap in the hedge or a place to collapse in terrified exhaustion. If these brutes had been dogs I would have been within my rights to shoot them, but all I could do in these instances was throw stones at their sainted paintwork, which I always did.

In the last years Turpin was a great help to me on road journeys. Not that he was capable of doing anything clever – he just stayed close to me and the sheep learned to ignore him – but because most motorists, alerted by television coverage to the superior brainpower of many border collies, slowed down when they saw him, so that they wouldn't miss a chance to see it in action.

But on that spring morning we were spared any real trouble. The ewes trudged one by one through the gate and into the field and I counted them in and made them secure. Still, I thought, as my dog and I went home for lunch, it would have been nice to have spotted just one sign of winter's end, with lambing time so near and all.

Last thing that night I began my spring ritual for what turned out to be the last time. Off came the slippers, on went thermal socks, wellingtons, donkey jacket and woolly hat; out into the dark I went, flashlight in hand, to check that all was well with the sheep.

As I was striding up the steep field behind the house, I caught sight of a movement on the ground, and when I shone the torch I couldn't prevent a little shiver of disgust before the feeling was overtaken by interest and wonder. The ground was a seething mass of worms. Worms in a frenzy of hermaphrodite reproduction. Worms reaching out to one another in a writhing carpet of togetherness, each one maintaining a tail-hold on its own burrow so that when they were picked out in the light beam they snapped back into safety like knicker elastic. Up the hill I continued, like an usherette illuminating the back row of the cinema stalls, while nature in the raw squirmed around my green and grubby boots.

All was well. No lambs, no problems. I was coming back across the open field at the top of the hill when a strange noise caught my attention. A rustle and a slurp. A sound like surreptitious gum-chewing in the silence of an examination room. I shone the flashlight. And there, taking full advantage of the warm, wet worms was a small and happy hedgehog feasting on live vermicelli.

Signs of spring, I decided with a grin, and I would do well to make the most of them. A strange wind had sprung up from the south, rough and almost hot, like dogs' breath, and I knew that it would be raining by morning.

It was a good, straightforward lambing. I had timed things well; I was there when I was needed. But as the year wore on it was not always so.

I inoculated all the lambs, marked them and turned them out on to the common with their mothers. As always I kept them in a day or two too long, dreading letting them go out of my sight, but I felt the usual surge of pride on the warm evening when I opened the moorgate and watched them go, the ewes heading up to the spaces on which I'd hefted them, dawdling and nibbling, while their lambs, besotted with the sudden space, bounced and capered alongside. The new red marks on their creamy fleeces – three apiece, shoulder, back and loin – made them look like Berwick cockles dropped by accident among the heather. This was the mark I had chosen for myself when I first began to keep Swaledale sheep and it was now known and recognized by all the farmers who turned sheep out on that mighty moor. I watched the column wind away and stayed watching long after they were out of sight, enjoying the familiar feelings of pride and responsibility and love.

Spring started rehearsing for summer. Time for moor flocks to fend for themselves. The routine tasks undertaken by my neighbours were as random and unpredictable as ever but now it was often impossible to contrive to be on hand to share in them. I realized that I minded very much that, if the moor was gathered without me, my sheep would be sorted and handled in my absence. I knew well enough that when Jim and George and the rest asked, 'What do you want doin' wi' thine, Missus?' whatever I requested would be faithfully carried out. In fact in my absence they would probably be spared even the jocular roughness which they suffered when I was present, it being directed more at me than at them. All the same I fretted like a parted lover and understood that there was more than a touch of jealousy in among the guilt.

One day Jim and George gathered the lower end of the moor to catch up with a few unmarked lambs and I called in on the way back from York to ask how it had gone. George told me that one of my ewes had refused to split off from his and he had let it down into his fields. 'She'll be right, Missus. She's got her lamb and they've both got their teeth and arseholes with 'em,' – and I took home with me his promise that he'd turn them out again along with his as soon as he'd marked his lambs.

As it happened that wasn't for some time. A crop of silage took up the next week or so. May God forgive me, it was almost that much later when I took a walk up the moor to see how things were going and found one of my lambs grazing alone. Pot-bellied and spindle-shanked it had quite clearly been weaned suddenly and too soon; its mother was nowhere to be seen. I took it home for special care, disappointed that the ewe, whom I knew to be a good and generous mother, had abandoned it. I looked for her but did not find her. I hoped she would turn up when we gathered the moor for shearing.

I met George some time later and he said, 'You'd better get a look at that lamb o' thine. It's mawked.'

I went with him and found my ewe and lamb in one of his buildings. He was right about the lamb; it was mawked – infested with blowfly maggots which had struck the soiled wool under its tail. It had been eating too much grass. George said, 'You'd better take a look at t'aud yow; she's not doing him too well,' and I sat her up and took a look at her udder. It was hot and swollen and the few drops I drew from her stank of putrefaction. She had mastitis. She was the mother, not of the lamb that George had incarcerated with her, but of the lamb I had found on the moor.

'Didn't you bother seeing if they mothered-up?' I shrieked at George who shouted back, 'Now don't start, Missus – I've got better things to do than run around doing thy job,' and more. Far more. I wept bitterly. Because George was shouting at me. Because he really should have taken the trouble, no matter whose sheep they were. Because a ewe and lamb of mine were suffering because I had trusted someone to do what I knew I should have done myself. And because I was bone-weary, confused, miserable and well on the way to being barking mad.

George probably felt guilty, too. It was his guilt that

made him say the cruel things he did, and mine that made me believe every word of them.

The mawked lamb rallied, along with the other one. The ewe's mastitis responded to antibiotics and she didn't lose a quarter. The other ewe, having been on the moor and on rougher keep, had dried up without trouble but I lay awake imagining four innocent voices raised in grief, crying out to the shepherd who had not heard any of them until it was too late.

Summer stumbled towards September. During the long vacation I revised the texts I had studied during the spring term, much of which I had spent joyfully in the School of Mediaeval Studies. In among the writings of those magical centuries I came upon wonderful neglected words to add to my vocabulary, which I look upon much as a philatelist does his album. It was among the alliterative literature of the period that I found one particular word – wanhope – that was much in my mind at that time.

One Tuesday, at eleven o'clock, I found myself sitting among the nettles at the edge of the road holding on to the hook end of a dog-lead, the other end of which was fastened in a slip-knot about the horns of one of my sheep. I had noticed that one of the young ewes had begun to look a little uncomfortable while awaiting her compulsory autumn dipping and that gradually, over the days that followed, she became downright ill.

Her skin blistered and split and the flies, still rampant in the warm autumn weather, were irresistibly attracted by the weeping sores on her back. I phoned the vet and described the symptoms. Instead of the usual reassuring answer came a small, meaningful silence.

'It sounds – only sounds, mind you – as though it could be scab.' His tone told me at once that he wasn't joking.

Ever practical, he suggested that I contact the Ministry and ask them to send one of their own vets out to take samples. That way, he suggested kindly, if it really did turn out to be the big S I wouldn't have to pay for the doubtful privilege of finding out. 'They've privatized everything else,' he said, gloomily, 'but I think they still accept some responsibility for our notifiable diseases.' As I thanked him a little too brightly and lowered the phone I heard him say, 'Good luck.'

I was going to need all the luck I could get. If it turned out that the poor little ewe had scab, which is a form of mange caused by a burrowing mite, like scabies in humans, it would mean that all my neighbours would have to gather in all the sheep they had so recently clipped, dipped and turned loose and dip them again, not once, but twice, under Ministry supervision and at a cost of hundreds of pounds. All movements would be forbidden, causing even more expense and inconvenience. I, whose image was already tarnishing, would be about as popular as the Reverend Paisley at Saint Peter's.

I felt groggy and weak. The day before I had had a general anaesthetic as part of a minor operation and the after-effects were producing strange waves of hallucination.

The Ministry vet had told me that he would come 'sometime during the morning' and I had determined to get the sheep down to the house and into a building before he came but I knew by the way my legs softened like cold spaghetti when I dragged her out of the field and on to the road that I hadn't the energy to chase her home, so I fished Turpin's lead out of my pocket, looped it round her horns and half drove, half dragged her halfway to the gate before collapsing in the nettles for a breather, which was where the man from the Ministry found the pair of us.

He took his samples there and then, scraping them from various parts of her afflicted surface. That done he asked questions, filled in forms, noted names and addresses and finally put into my hand the terrible piece of paper that forbade movement of my sheep until such time as the ban was officially lifted.

I had arranged to take all my wether lambs to market next day, move the gimmers down to the house and turn the ewes back to the common. Now the lambs would have to stay where they were and the ewes would have to stay on their exhausted pasture and without the sale of the lambs how would I buy in fodder for them?

I went back home and fetched a jar of ointment – an old-fashioned emollient coupled with an up-to-date fly repellent. At least I could make the sheep feel better. My legs throbbed, my feet hurt and my heart ached. That was when I remembered the word – wanhope.

In the glossary at the back of the book it was translated as 'despair' but suddenly I knew better. Wanhope is something far more terrible than despair. Wanhope is hope itself, in a grubby raincoat, seen from behind. Leaving.

13
Levelling the Sand-castle

I suppose it's like a child building a sand-castle. This is
the best and biggest sand-castle I've ever built. And I can
see the sea coming in. But if anybody's going to break it
down, it'll be me – you know – I'll stamp on it first. . . .

From an interview for Yorkshire Television
Calendar Tuesday, Spring 1984

Did I really know as long ago as 1984 that what I had made
was doomed? Probably. Live television, like wine, has a
way of producing truth that may surprise in retrospect.

I picked the wrong simile, that was all. I had imagined a
sand-castle, going slowly and with a degree of dignity; I
saw myself in control, with time to choreograph the process
so that the end itself was part of the story, smoothing itself
clean and flat.

What I had ended up with, though, was not a sand-castle at all but a Prince Rupert's Drop, and its destiny was
built into the shape of it. To keep safe the farm and the
dream it represented, I had frozen it small and safe in a

glass globe, so that I could set it on a sort of mental win-dow-sill in my absences and come back to it, finding it safe and unchanged. As I distanced myself from it more often and in more ways, the globe that held it underwent a change. It was still there but now it hung at the end of a stiff stalk, pulled out long and thin from it like hot glass dripped into cold water. The globe itself was hard and invulnerable to hammer blows; its weak point was the fragile stalk, the slightest injury to which would shatter it to powder. I had tried so hard to preserve it intact but with inappropriate emphasis on the preciousness of home. In the end it was a relatively small snag at the thin end of the long tail that broke everything apart.

It turned out not to be sheep scab after all. The ewe, newly sheared, appeared to have been suffering from pho-tosensitivity, probably brought about by an allergy to some of the pasture weeds which were almost the only surviving vegetation in the field where they had stayed too long wait-ing to be included in the bi-annual compulsory dipping. Access at last to the open moor with unlimited bent-grass and bilberries soon effected a cure.

Each time I returned home something had changed. Not necessarily for worse or better; just changed. It was as though my parallel lives were themselves alive, like mov-ing pavements. I suppose I had assumed, in a human sort of way, that it was my stepping on or off that stopped and started them. One night there was a touch of the Gothic about my home-coming that accorded oddly with my changing frame of mind.

As soon as I came into the house I could feel that some-thing unusual had happened. It was too quiet, as though some frantic activity had suddenly ceased as my arrival altered the balance of the scene. When I turned on the light it took a moment or two for my eyes to adjust; at first there seemed to be a grey, undulating film on the carpet but as I looked it resolved itself into a gentle drift of feathers, quivering slightly in the draught from the door. A cat had clearly been up to no good in my absence.

The door to my bedroom was ajar. I went through to see what might have been left there for me. A body, perhaps, or a fistful of muddled entrails. A glance round the room showed me nothing new. Of the red, wet ruins of wren or robin there was no sign. Relieved, I pushed the door shut behind me. There came a shriek as a battered black bird which had been recuperating on top of the door after its hairs-breadth escape from Mrs Willoughby was skittled from its perch as the door slid beneath the lintel.

I don't think it quoth 'nevermore'; I can only say that it hit the back of my neck like a warm, wet sponge before grabbing with its skinny feet at the shoulder of my jersey, where it clung, flopping. I detached it carefully, folded it tidily and held it safe between my hands while I examined it. It looked just the way I felt. Crestfallen, ruffled and defeated.

The university course had suddenly become much harder. I was now studying the Romantic period and found that something inexplicable had happened to the happy kaleidoscope between my ears that had hitherto served me for a brain. I could no longer contribute in seminars because I found I could not adapt the thoughts in my head into a form that would be comprehensible to the company in which I now found myself and, worse, I could not grasp what it was that they were saying in response to the literature we were studying. There was a whole new language in use and I was not familiar with it. It was a code; thoughts and questions voiced *en clair* sounded naïve and ridiculous and were for the most part kindly ignored.

That day I had sat listening to a discussion of a poem by Goethe which described an apple tree overhanging the edge of a lake and my head had just snapped off and floated away, like a cheap balloon from an inattentive market trader. It mattered overwhelmingly that I had never seen or heard of an apple tree growing alongside water. I didn't think it would be suited to such a habitat. I longed to ask if anyone else had seen one. Presumably Goethe had. Was it some age-related prejudice that made me want to challenge his observation? I'd have believed John Clare or even, at a pinch, William Barnes. Perhaps the tree was high up on a sort of cliff . . . I made a half-hearted grab for my head but it refused to come back. It was away now, bobbing against the high windows, looking out across lawns all covered in seasonal goose-shit as though it could see backwards to Kent . . . childhood trips . . . oasthouses . . . orchards with no lakes in them . . . I was asked a question and could not respond. . .

A dull resignation to my own inadequacy settled on me like a drowsy numbness. I had lost the power to criticize; I could only carp and copy. I had opinions, sure, but I had lost the power to express them cogently. Or perhaps I never had it. Perhaps I was cursed with a superficiality of attitude that would prevent me from ever penetrating the deeper groves of academe. I was too tired to care.

I felt the hurt bird move in my hand and realized that I had been holding it far too tightly.

During the next few days I applied for, and was granted, compassionate leave from my studies, so that I could recapture my head and reinforce the threadbare places in the rest of me.

But what could I do? To come home and stay in that changed place, to pick up the pieces of a dream I'd patched and adapted until it broke, would probably destroy me. To wind down the farm and just live in the house in the rubble of the dream would finish me just as surely. To be there on the periphery of it all, an observer, a stranger without a stake in it, would be a special kind of hell.

I decided to leave the farm. To leave it by going away from it, by being somewhere else, and to leave it by letting it be, letting it settle like cooling cinders into whatever form it might take behind the closing door.

I talked it over with the children and they gave their blessing. They came home and took from the place the things they needed to keep for themselves and I promised to pack up and keep for them anything they felt they might need later. Nan adopted the kitten, Cocoon, taking her to share her flat in Northallerton. Robert took down his posters and boxed his books. Andy sorted through his things and left me in charge of a single cardboard box, labelled 'my life'.

I thought of going to Wales, because of the distance and the newness of it, both of which would challenge and distract, and because of the samenesses, which would comfort me.

I gave away most of the livestock to other smallholders whom I trusted to care in the same way I did. Geese, poultry and pet lambs, the jersey heifer and the one last pig. I left most of the equipment for Jim.

The sheep I sold as a flock in the autumn sale at Northallerton. I could have taken them to Hawes or

Swainby, but I owed Peter the auction manager that small
compliment in return for the many times he'd let me work
as a drover when I needed the money and let me off paying
commission when I couldn't afford it.

I felt strange at the sale. I was playing the market drover
for the very last time. I brought my own sheep up into the
pen behind the ring and then stepped into shepherd mode,
going in with them through the doors. I sold them in three
lots; the hoggs, the ewes and the shearlings. These last, the
young ewes ready to go to the tup for the first time, made
the top price of the day. I was proud because this was a gen-
uine compliment to my shepherding, a justification of so
many years of hard work. I picked up my money from the
office, left a little 'luck' for the buyers and went home to a
silence that nearly broke my heart.

Fat Frank hired a van and drove us to Wales. Me, Mrs
Willoughby, Dylan and Turpin, who snored ecstatically at
my feet, utterly relaxed, it not mattering to him where we
were going, because we were going together.

Epilogue

Like all good metaphors (and all good pigs) the pig in the passage can be worked to the very last whisker. Her relentless foward motion is that of Heraclitus' river, she is Spenser's mutabilitee made flesh. As it were.

She is indefatigable, like the Green Knight, but equally without malice. Because she is a pig, the sort of injuries you get from trying to impede her progress are not life-threatening. Cowards get trapped against the wall, heroes are simply upskittled and trodden on. The treading hurts; the pig is very heavy but her feet are very small. Thus the pressure they exert, when given in pounds per square inch, is phenomenal. Especially vulnerable are the toes and the heart.

When I found out, under field conditions, that I could neither stop the pig nor stand the pain, the only option left was to jump on her back, hang on to her ears and go with her through the door. So I did.